My Father never Wanted
us to **First Cut** Watch
Memoirs of a football
football··· **fan** £3·84·
Ordered on 15 August 2022.
Remember 15 Aug. 1987. Tunde.
Lot Danai Chitakasha (Football)
Oluyemisi Ade Jaiyesimi·
198 Southend Road·

**DEAN
THOMPSON**

Stanford- le – hope·
South Publishing Essex·

**DEAN
THOMPSON**

Publishing

Essex, United Kingdom

First Cut: Memoirs of a football fan

First published in Great Britain in 2020 by Dean Thompson Publishing

ISBN: 9798661266613

Dedication

I would like to dedicate this book to my wife Tendai and my son Tinashe who have supported me throughout this project. I will not forget to mention my brothers Saul, Edward, Clement "Chopelo", Simba, Abedinigo and my sisters Violet and Ngaakudzwe who made my childhood experiences so rich that I incorporated those memories into this story.

To my late father, Mudhara Abisha who never wanted us to watch football, tough, but a man of principles and my late mother Joyce your good works live on. What we do to and for those around us, those we meet and live with everyday, are seeds that germinate and bear fruits in our lives, for the powerful lesson, I thank you mom Dora. Thank you for the love!

Acknowledgements

The contributions of many people have made this book a reality.

First, I thank God and I hold on to the word "For with God all things are possible". This message has kept me going.

I thank my wife Tendai who has pushed me to complete the project and also my son Tinashe who has always been ready with an encouraging word. I thank my good old friend Dr. Francis Garaba, we have been together since 1985 and all these years he has always encouraged me to put my football experiences on paper. I started off by writing articles for online newspapers, but he was not content with that. He kept pushing me until I took heed. He literally planted the seed, watered it until it germinated. I am sure he will enjoy reading this book, he is a football man!

I want to thank Lance Guma, the Editor of Nehanda Radio who showed confidence in me and gave me space on his paper to reach a wider audience. The feedback that I got from the articles grew my confidence and I built a reputation as an authority on Zimbabwe Football. Welton Shoriwa is a respected authority on Zimbabwe football history and from him I learnt a lot. He reminded me about so many dates and events which I had forgotten. Thank you Welton for not being stingy with information. Your help is much cherished.

I thank Freddy Pasuwa Mugadza posthumously, the man we all knew as The Chairman. He passed on before the publication of this book, cruel fate! His Facebook page, The Freddy Pasuwa Football Page, is a rich source of football knowledge from which I generously borrowed some ideas. I also had to borrow several pictures and for that, I want to thank Zimpapers for their rich archives. Many pictures were also borrowed from the now defunct flagship magazines like Parade and Horizon, I take this opportunity to acknowledge them. It is such a shame that these are no more but while they existed they were a rich source of football news and photos.

I thank legend Francis Nechironga. I have known him since 1982 and he shared with me intimate information on his football experiences. I learnt a lot from our football discussions.

I would also want to thank Albert Marufu who gave me ideas on how to take the next step into publishing. Legend Japhet "Shortcat" Mparutsa was always available with advice and legend Cephas "Mai Chisamba," Chimedza, thank you for writing the foreword. This is much appreciated.

Last, but not least, I want to acknowledge Itayi Garande of Dean Thompson Publishing for helping me with this publication. Thank you for the excellent work.

Sisonke!

Foreword
By Cephas "Mai Chisamba, Mboma" Chimedza
(Dynamos, Caps United, Sint Truidenese of Belgium)

I have always considered myself the lucky one because I stopped playing football before the advent of social media. Facebook was just taking of and it was not for everyone. I remember after one match, I went home and unfriended many fans who I thought had booed me during the match and continued to do so on Facebook.

The influence of social media has grown over the years and as an "old fashioned guy" I often wonder how current players cope with the relentless attention. Sometimes I get angry when I read about fans having a go at the players for having a bad match. I have however come to accept the power of social media and have begun to glean some positives. Fans are now able to interact with their heroes and documenting of events and records is now very easy.

Not a day passes without some fans talking to me about my football career, everyday someone wants to know how I got my nicknames and how I was cheeky enough to kiss the ball. What was I thinking? I just laugh but through this interaction, the history is not lost unlike in the days of old when the events are easily forgotten.

In Zimbabwe, we have a problem with the keeping of records. The exploits of past football heroes before the advent of social media have been lost. Very few journalists and writers have made an effort to retrieve these and write books to keep the memories alive. It is therefore refreshing to come across a person like Lot Danai

Chitakasha who has vast knowledge of Zimbabwe football history from the 1980's.

I have known Lot Danai from his many football articles online, which are always rich in content, and I am glad that he has taken a step further to write a book. He has a passion for Zimbabwe football and his knowledge of players, matches and events in our football terrain is expansive.

Reading his book has made aware that Lot Danai is a proper football person. He has put his vast knowledge to good use. The book takes the reader on a journey, a journey full of drama proving once more that the Zimbabwe football terrain is rich and has lot that can be explored. His loyalty to the Zimbabwe league, Caps United, and our football heroes is unwavering and comes out clearly in this book. In addition, Yes Lot Danai still thinks that Joel Shambo is the greatest midfielder to ever grace our local stadiums. Well, I will not argue with him!

Well done Lot Danai, we need more documentation of our football history.

Usanete!

The Author – Lot Danai Chitakasha

Lot Danai Chitakasha is a veteran football writer and biographer who is passionate about Zimbabwe Football. In 2016, together former Dynamos, Black Rhinos and Zimbabwe National Team goalkeeper, Japhet "Shortcat" Mparutsa, Lot broke new ground by co-authoring the Legend's autobiography, *Japhet "Shortcat" Mparutsa, My Story*. This was pioneering work in Zimbabwe Football history since no local football player apart from Bruce Grobbelaaar who was based in Europe, had ever put their story on paper. The biography was a great success. Lot Chitakasha, who worked for many years as an educationist in Zimbabwe, now lives and works in the United Kingdom with Tendai, his wife of twenty-seven years and their son Tinashe. He holds a Bachelor of Arts degree in English and History, a PGCE from the University of Zimbabwe and a CELTA certification from Cambridge.

Chapter 1
The first cut!

I departed the village with a heavy heart! I had just finished my primary education at St Andrews Primary school, Rusape in 1980 and now I had go to Harare for my secondary education. It was heartbreaking to leave my grandmother behind since she had become like a mother to me. I had developed a strong bond with Mbuya Mutsvuku, a name she had earned because she was very light in complexion. Now I had to leave because my father who had remarried after many years as a widower, wanted us to be together and as he put it in his own words, "bond and become one family again."

Mbuya Mutsvuku, was strict, but fair. She believed in hardwork and above everything else, she believed in the work of her hands. Even after so many years, I can still hear the echo of her voice in her Manyika accent, "Handidiba vanhu vanogarira maoko!" which literally means "… i do not want people to sit on their hands!" This was a kind of refrain for her, a mantra that she drummed it in us day in and day out. She expected my brother and I to contribute to household chores.

So, from an early age, we learnt all the basics, preparing the fire, cooking sadza, cleaning up after ourselves, looking after the chickens, closing them in and opening to allow them to roam the homestead in search of food. And of cause when Mbuya's favourite cow Mariposa gave birth, we learnt how to milk it too. Mariposa was generous with her milk and I remember well the nourishing yoghurt we made from her bountiful milk. We were spoilt and though we had to spend time in the fields,

1

weeding when there was weeding to be done and harvesting when we had to harvest, it was all good fun.

She trained us well! "I do not want you to grow up into lazy layabouts who cannot look after themselves," Mbuya Mutsvuku extolled the virtues of hard work with the zeal of a missionary. The villagers respected her for this, hardworkers consulted her for ideas while the lazy disliked her but never stayed away from her. Widowed at an early age, she had to fend for herself and four daughters after the death of her husband. She did not remarry, instead she became an integral member of the Mushayi family and stayed on to raise her children. When her children grew up and got married, she then took some of the grandchildren to raise them up. This is how I came to live with Mbuya Mutsvuku.

My mother died when I was only nine leaving behind six children. Death when it came did not exactly come like a thief because by the time she died she had been ill for a long time. As children, we were too young to understand death, and when it came, it dislocated the family. Fortunately, the strength of our African culture came to the fore as the children were quickly adopted by various relatives. I went to live with my aunt, Tete Loice in a village called Muziti.

Tete was a strong woman but she also had her own heartbreak to deal with. Her husband had disappeared leaving her with two children to look after. He went to Zambia to look for work and never came back. "Muchoni" is all we heard about him, meaning "the one who went and never came back". However, Tete Loice stayed on, waited and waited in hope. She died aged around eighty years, the husband she waited for a distant memory of what could have been. Although she was married, she had lived her whole life like a single woman with only the company of her two children Stephen and Dorothy as reminders of her early years of marital bliss. How cruel can life be?

Then the raging war of liberation reached Muziti village. Somehow the Rhodesia soldiers thought our primary school was a potential recruiting ground for what Ian Smith used to call "terrorists" but the ones we called "vanamukoma", the comrades. The inevitable befell us when in the summer of 1977, they closed the school. With no school to attend, my father soon came and whisked me away to Madziwa village. In this village, the war had not reached its peak so the nearest primary school, St Andrews was operating at full throttle.

Madziwa village was an oasis of calm although some ten kilometres away in Mawango village the comrades had arrived. Gunfire, the hovering helicopters and death were not uncommon there. We heard all about this but never fully experienced it. Well, until one day when the comrades came in the middle of the night and asked all the villagers to gather at the Sabhuku's homestead.

The mandatory slogan chanting "Pamberi nehondo, Pamberi nekubatana, Pamberi ne Zanu," which means "Forward with war, forward with unity, forward with Zanu !" which we had to learn on the spot followed. They told us to contribute to the war effort by destroying the cattle dipping facility in the village. It was deemed to be a symbol of the oppressive Ian Smith government.

As kids, we enjoyed going to the dip tank with our cattle but now the comrades told us that this was a bad thing. A new war consciousness was being cultivated in us! We complied and the following night we gathered some rocks, both small and big ones which we dumped in the dip. We destroyed the roofing and left the place in an unrecognisable state. When the revenge of the regime soldiers came, it was ruthless. They gathered the cattle they could find in the village and shot them, "If you cannot dip the cattle, you will not keep them!" They said.

Mbuya Mutsvuku was lucky. Her cattle had already gone to the pastures and so escaped the carnage. Not so tete Ndofeni, a strong-willed woman of the village who lived on her own, she lost eight of her beasts and was left inconsolable. This was the cost of war and we felt it. After that, they asked us to take out all the rocks. The dilemma of war was that the villagers were left stuck between a hard rock and the deep sea though it was all for the cherished goal of freedom. And yes, freedom eventually did come!

At Mbuya Mutsvuku's, I grew up together with my young brother Clement and my elder brother Edward. As earlier stated, the message of hardwork never departed from her lips. She eschewed indolence, and from the villagers she had many examples to draw from. Like Mai Tafirenyika, her lady neighbour who had four children. Her husband worked for the road department and only came home once every year at Christmas.

Mai Tafirenyika complained endlessly about the neglect that she suffered from her irresponsible man whose only understanding of his duties as a husband was to make her pregnant. Other than that, he cared little about how she looked after the brood of children he bestowed upon her. Mbuya gave Mai Tafirenyika the same advice that she gave everyone, "Usagarire maoko, do not sit on your hands!" Her advice however fell on rocky ground, Mai Tafirenyika was the perennial moaner and beggar.

Then there was Sekuru Muteedzanzira, so named because he never spent time in the fields. He used to wake up, take a bath, put on his Sunday best attire even on a Monday and head to the shops for a pint of his favourite beer. He had spent his time in Salisbury, the capital city where he had worked and so had a bit of money to spend from his pension fund. When everyone was in the fields doing some back breaking work, he would be in one of the bottle stores which littered our local shopping centre, KwaMatiza as we called the place, chatting up the storekeeper, usually a young lady.

4

Mbuya Mutsvuku was far from impressed, she railed against such behaviour, "What kind of person is that, his back never bends down?" she would ask rhetorically. "Do not envy such people otherwise poverty will be your companion...!" she warned us wearing that stern look on her face which she always deployed whenever she wanted to drive her point home.

She reserved her vitriolic for another interesting character of our village, sekuru Hwami. Sekuru Hwami was the senior bachelor of the village, a lovable rogue but a pet hate for Mbuya. He lived with his mother, an old lady who did all the household chores while he indulged his twin passions, gambling and attending beer parties. Gambling was anathema to Mbuya Mutsvuku and she warned us strongly against such behaviour. Every weekend, Sekuru Hwami would find an excuse to join any beer party, which happened to be taking place in the village, and these were many. He was not always invited, but he had a way of inviting himself.

There was a trick he was never tired of using, "I heard a bit of noise here and thought, 'let me see what is going lest I pass by leaving people fighting'." He introduced himself thus but of course, he knew people were not fighting. They were having a good time and he had to join in to quench his seemingly insatiable thirst. Fellow villagers were now familiar with this old trick and would welcome him. They immediately handed over the beer-sharing duties to him. They loved his endless tales of adventure as he dished the frothy seven days brew, but Mbuya Mutsvuku was never amused.

She reminded us, "Do not be like Hwami, a man who cannot look after his own mother, a man who will not marry so that his mother can have a helper, puu!!", she said spitting into the dying ambers of the evening fire.

My brothers and I listened and the more she spoke against sekuru Hwami's twin evils of beer chasing and gambling, the more we became determined to stay on the narrow and straight. "When Hwami dies, he will be buried with a rat in his grave because he does not want to get married!" Mbuya deployed the cultural dimension to the lessons of our childhood. Who would like to be buried in the company of a rat in his grave? That was an abomination, so to marry became one of our goals as we grew up! And marry we eventually did, it came much later.

Life in the village was fun despite the rumblings of war and the regular visits by the Smith regime soldiers who constantly asked "Arikupi Gandanga, where are the terrorists?" To this, we had been trained to give one firm answer, "We do not know, we have not seen them!" Any other answer was an invitation of trouble, the comrades would accuse you of selling out.

The war situation never dimmed our enjoyment of life, a life of plenty, peaches, yams, potatoes and the wild fruits too. We formed strong bonds in the village, friendships which lasted a life time. On my part I was truly and well immersed in village life, my heart, mind and soul were in the village. I simply loved it. I went to school, played football with friends but never got into the school team. Together with friends, we cheered with gusto, singing by the touchline for those that were good enough to represent us as they fought the battles on the rocky pitch.

The teachers had no other coaching technique apart from using the cane or whip every time someone failed to control the ball. For this reason, I avoided getting involved, preferring instead to be part of the cheering students. When the election results were announced in 1980, I was in Grade Seven. We knew that independence had come, and we joined the celebrations.

Leaving Mbuya Mutsvuku behind therefore was not easy, it was heart wrenching. Saying goodbye to my friends was even more difficult. It felt like a part of me was dying. But my father insisted that we had to go to Harare and so for Harare we departed, my brother excited as I wore a sad long face, I did not want to leave!

The Harare I landed in had recently transformed itself from Salisbury and like the rest of the country was under the grip of the independence fervour. Zimbabwe was one year old, independence was a culmination of a long war, a war which I had caught a glimpse of in the village with that dipping facility adventure. Now everyone was happy that the war was over.

Excitement was in the air. The shackles of oppression had been shaken off, the oppressive white settler regime which discriminated on race was finally defeated. We danced to songs of freedom. In 1981, Thomas Mapfumo sang the song "Chitima Cherusununguko, The Freedom Train." While Harare Mambos Band released, "Mbuya Nehanda Kufa vachitaura, tora gidi uzvitonge, take the gun and rule yourself'. The whole atmosphere was electric and charged with emotional patriotism.

Indeed, we were ready to rule ourselves. The freedom train had arrived! Harare was the place to be. The new government promised great things. We had total faith in the new leadership which was hailed as the most educated in Africa.

The new nation was on an upward trajectory. We were full of hope. Reality later sank in, but that was many years down the line, when the train derailed. For that time, we basked in the glory of freedom, for that flirting moment we looked forward to a great future!

Despite my earlier reservations, I took to Harare like a duck to water. I settled in Jerusalem, a section of the sprawling township of Highfield where my father's house was located. I enrolled at a new school, made new friends and enrolled at the nearby library. Gwanzura stadium, the second largest football stadium at the time, was just a stone's throw away! Then it happened – my football baptism of fire and what a way to become a fan!

My new step-mother had a young sister, Mainini Levies, who loved football and decided to take me to Gwanzura Stadium for a match. There we were, I had no clue which teams were playing, I just saw one in green and another in shiny yellow. The yellow uniform which turned out to be Black Aces looked attractive to me and my heart was captured. It was the folly of youth! I was only fourteen and was easily impressionable. My aunt did not seek to explain anything, she just settled into her seat and waited for the magic to unfold. Hey! The magic indeed unfolded, the green team attacked from all angles.goals flew in and they seemed to score every time they attacked. When the referee blew his whistle to end proceedings, the yellow team had long accepted defeat. This turned up to be a humiliation, my first step into football fandom had started on a false note.

My yellow team had been massacred and through all this my aunt said nothing. From the way she was smiling and jumping about, I knew she was in the other camp and her team in green was delivering the goods in a spectacular fashion. Only when we got home did she say, "That was Caps United son, they train at the Zimbabwe Grounds, you should go and watch them."

I needed no second persuasion!

That was the beginning of my journey, it became a daily pilgrimage for me to go and watch the team train. Caps United became my team and I knew all the players. Forty years later, I still remember the players that I saw training at the Zimbabwe grounds in 1981, Obediah Sarupinda, Ashton Nyazika were the coaches, David Gwanzura, Size Torindo, William Chikauro, Batsirai Jambwa, Charles Sibanda, Clever Muzuva, Joel Shambo, Stix Mtizwa, Stanley Ndunduma, Shacky Tauro, Friday Phiri, Tobias Moyo, Oliver Chidemo, Francis Nechironga, Takaitei Muswe, Todd Chitimbe, Dixon Nwenya and John Lauro, Emmanuel Mhlanga and many other junior players.

They were a team full of stars with Shambo, Mtizwa, Tauro, Ndunduma and Friday Phiri as the big stars. A few years later in 1983, I was heartbroken when the team lost stars, Stanley Ndunduma and William Chikauro to a newly formed army team Black Rhinos. Stanford "Stix" Mtizwa the talented midfield star followed later in 1984, another big blow. I could not eat for weeks but thank God for Joel Shambo, he stayed and helped the team to rebuild.

My love for the team never wavered over the years, it grew from strength to strength. This first generation of players whom I watched were later followed by others who wore the green jersey with pride. The team was especially good in cup competitions. I remember them dominating the Zifa Castle Cup which was the premier knockout competition in the country. They won it in 1980, I did not watch this match, 1981, 1982 and 1983 and for that the Cup Kings tag was firmly attached to them.

As fans we were thrilled by these cup wins but the one we craved, the League Championship was elusive. I had missed the team's only title in 1979, at the time I was still in the rural areas oblivious of anything that was happening in the world of football. In 1996 this all changed when the team struck gold! The team clinched its first league championship after independence with a blend of attacking football which made rivals green with envy and made supporters go to bed with a smile on their faces. What a group of players these were, George Mudiwa, Charles Johane, Mpumelelo Dzvova, Joe Mugabe, captain Silver Chigwenje, Frank Nyamukuta, Lloyd Chitembwe, Mr Pefect Farai Mbidzo with his inch perfect passes, and the attacking quartet of Stewart Murisa, Alois Bunjira, Morgan Nkatazo and Simon Dambadza from the bench, all contributed to make us happy.

The brand Caps United continued to grow with further successes in the league in 2004, 2005 and 2016. I am glad that I remain a committed and loyal member of this Green family. There have been lows too, but the good memories are cherished, I am forever grateful to my aunt for taking me to that first encounter, I found my love!

It was also with Caps United that I watched one of the best matches ever at Rufaro Stadium. The year 1987, the trophy, the beautiful Chibuku trophy, the opponents a star studded Black Rhinos Football club which had former Caps United favourites Stanley Ndunduma, Stix Mtizwa and William Chikauro in their arsenal. Two matches were played, the first one i call it "The Thriller at Rufaro!".

It ended three to three, what a game this was. For as long as I live, I will never forget this football match. It is generally accepted as the match of the 80's. Unfortunately, the replay which was nearly as good, did not bring the desired result for me, my team lost by two goals to one. Heartbreak for me but I always comfort myself with the first match, The Thriller at Rufaro!

And yes, Gwanzura Stadium became pivotal and central to the development of my football journey. I have unforgettable memories of this old stadium, good memories and sad ones too. For most young people, it became a rites of passage, to be a Highfield boy and be accepted as such, one had to embark on all the adventures and misadventures associated with this stadium. Match days were special. We scaled the precast wall to gain entrance into the stadium.

"Kupoya," we called it.

Woe to those who were caught by the security guards who were always in the company of vicious dogs. Many boys have nasty experiences with these dogs Many still carry scars of these battles! The less brave opted to call out at the gates, "Pano Pakavhurwa. It is open here!" and after facilitating the entrance of twenty people, the cashier would allow one boy in. The rest had to tout some more until their chance to get in came by. This only happened when the less popular teams were playing, with the big teams, there was no need to tout, the crowds were massive and everyone was in a hurry to get in.

On such days, there was another trick we used. We waited for the players to disembark from their team buses then offer to carry their kit bags. If a legend agreed, the lucky boy's entrance into the stadium through the VIP gate was guaranteed. Yes sometimes, when the bags of tricks ran out, we reluctantly parted with the savings of the week and paid to get into the stadium. However, sometimes, we waited outside for the last fifteen minutes of free entry, we called it the "VIP Treatment". We watched for fifteen minutes and still talked about the match as if we had watched the whole ninety minutes. The creativeness of youth!

At the end of matches, we poured onto the pitch to hug the players. We were glad to jump on their backs, rub off their sweat and yes, some naughty boys would take an opportunity to pinch the players, just to see their reaction. White players like Duncan Ellison of Caps United and Graham Boyle of Rio Tinto knew this well. The young boys wanted to pinch the white players to see if they could bleed. Sometimes, I just laugh as I go down memory lane! The folly of youth, "Kutswinya varungu, pinching the white players!" That was funny. This, however, established a good rapport with the players. We knew them well. We waited for them to shower and change then cheer them as they departed for their homes. I remember one day after a match rising star Moses Chunga emerged from the dressing room.

"Mhozeee, Mhozeee!" a group of young boys shouted.

He was so popular and as he walked to Machipisa shopping centre to get a lift to his home in Glen Norah, the young boys simply followed behind him – twenty to thirty young boys all walking behind Moses Chunga, just happy to be near. It was a royal escort until he boarded one of those old taxis which used to ply the Machipisa to

11

Glen Norah route. Those were the days! They were big stars, but they belonged to us. We loved them!

Gwanzura Stadium was also the scene of one of my saddest moments. One day we were playing football on the pitch. The caretaker, Mudhara Huna, used to allow us some hours on the pitch after matches. We organised ourselves into teams for an impromptu game of football. I went for a hard tackle on my friend, Happy Mudehwe. He was not happy. He wanted to fight. I did not want to fight. I backed off and hoped that someone would come between us and stop the fight from developing.

This was naive thinking on my part because boys will be boys. They wanted to see the fight. I had no choice, but to engage Happy. I threw a punch, it was the punch of a coward, I put all my strength into it. Boom, it landed on my friend's mouth and with the impact one of his tooth came flying out.

He felt it. He stopped.

"Vandikwadza, you have hurt me!" he said feeling the gaping hole in his mouth. Everyone gathered around, they had to find the tooth. Superstition! We believed that a lost tooth had to be found otherwise my friend would lose some more in the course of his life. We looked for it in the dusk and eventually found it. He took it, put it in his pocket. We hugged, friends again now regretting why we had fought at all, but the damage had been done. The incident still haunts me to this day. I regret it. It is one bad Gwanzura Stadium memory that I will carry to my grave. Though this is a bad memory, watching Caps United triumph over Black Aces that sunny afternoon became the first cut and they say, "The first cut is the deepest!"

My heart has been green ever since. My football outlook is global, but if truth be told, Caps United introduced me to the joy of football. My eyes might wonder abroad, enticed by clubs afar like Arsenal, Liverpool, Manchester or Barcelona but the attachment is not the same, the true attachment will always be Caps United and by extension the Zimbabwe League. It is the Zimbabwe Football League which made me a fan. For forty years, I have remained loyal, I still follow it closely even from a distance. The love is undimmed!

Caps United courted me. The Zimbabwe League provided the arena for me to develop this love. With such great teams like Dynamos, Highlanders, Gweru United, Ziscosteel, Rio Tinto, Zimbabwe Saints, Eagles, Bata Power, Arcadia, Black Mambas, Black Aces and many others I became acquainted. These teams had great players and no matter which team came to Gwanzura Stadium, we were assured of high quality matches. I became acquainted with most of the players and many of them left a lasting impression on my football mind. My love for the game grew. My knowledge of players developed. I became some kind of football expert even from such an early age. The highs, the lows, the celebrations and the heartbreaks the became part of football DNA.

With friends, we discussed football. We lived and breathed football and football became our life. I can declare without a shred of doubt that Caps United and, by extension, the Zimbabwe League will always be my first love.

Dear reader, allow me to share my experiences, I call them "First Cut! Memoirs of a football Fan"

Chapter 2
Rubbing shoulders with football greats – an early start!

"There are no places left at Highfields High school, so we have to try St. Peters Kubatana!", mother who had taken it upon herself to find a Form I place for me said. She tried to sound positive, I trusted her though I could sense her apprehension.

Yes, St. Peters Kubatana, because Highfield High school, everyone's school of choice was oversubscribed. St. Peters Kubatana, a school which had the Highfields Cemetry as its neighbour, was considered by many as the graveyard of any schooling ambitions. The students had a reputation for bad behaviour and the teachers were mostly unqualified. My new mother had to be at her motivational best, "You just have to make the best of it, there is no substitute for hard work," She said giving me an assuring pat on the head. I decided to believe her!

I was young, I was carefree but the reputation of my prospective school kept nagging at the back of my head. Highfield High school was the most sought-after school in the suburb, followed by Mukai High School and to some extent Kwayedza. St. Peters and Highfield Mhuriimwe, the so-called community schools were cruelly referred to as "Bamba zonke" literally translated as collect all! The cruel street commentators would say "collect all chaf, the no hopers." They were the schools for those who had not done so well at Grade seven. Even those students who had been expelled from other schools for misbehaviour would come to these schools to continue with their mischief. I remember Ticha, expelled from Goromonzi High school for nocturnal activities of beer drinking at the nearest

14

Growth point who came to St. Peters to finish his O levels. He was a handful, but I am going ahead of my story.

And so to St Peters I followed behind my stepmother, past Tsungai, Nyandoro and Mutasa primary schools, that cemetery where all the dead in Highfield lay rested, through the black painted gates at the school to the administration block. The admission process was surprisingly easy, the bespectacled Deputy Head did not even ask for my results slip. "We still have space for two more classes, just go and pay your fees at the reception," he said nonchalantly. His name was Mr. Chifamba. True to form, the receptionist also showed little interest in me as a student, she simply asked for the fees, scribbled quickly on the slip and handed me the receipt. No welcome, no words of encouragement, just the perfunctory nod and a "next" to the student behind me.

With the fees paid, we collected the uniform voucher, list of books and headed straight for the city centre. Grey shirt, grey short, grey socks, black shoes and the mandatory satchel completed the ritual of enrolling at my new school. By now the apprehension was fast dissipating, I was looking forward to my new life as a student with an upcoming new term that promised to be exciting.

The school was unique, it was two schools in one, the so-called community section and the F2 section. Both sections focused on the traditional subjects but also emphasised the practical ones. Building, carpentry, music especially marimba-playing and agriculture were top priority. There was also technical college which enrolled the students soon after they completed their O level studies. In 1982, the two sections merged into one, the student population was massive, the teachers as earlier stated were not the most qualified, but we managed. School was fun, the reputation about St. Peters was proving to be an exaggerated myth. But there were a few students who were determined to perpetuate the infamy, students like John Chinembiri, what an apt name. He was famous for the wrong reasons. He literally broke all the rules that one can imagine at a school, bullying, skipping lessons, smoking and when the teachers tried to discipline him, he simply refused.

There was another one called Minister, the students feared him, he was the type that used to come into a classroom and give everyone some claps. The teachers did nothing about it because they also feared Minister. The school kept such students on board because it had a non-expulsion policy believing as it did, that every student had a chance to reform and learn something. Generally, however, the atmosphere was good and indeed we enjoyed our time as students.

With time, I began to know more about the teachers and the supporting staff at the school. Lo and behold, history was unfolding right in front of my eyes! We went for a music lesson and guess who stood in front of us fine tuning our voices, none other than Jawett Nechironga, the free scoring striker for St. Pauls Musami Football Club, the Rhodesia League Champion of 1966. He was still in top shape, fit and bouncing and he spent most of the lessons telling us about his football exploits for the 1966 Champions. "We played football for passion, we did not care about the financial rewards", he reminisced.

We enjoyed the journey into the past even as he fine tuned our voices for the National Choir competitions. For a man of such football stature, it was a surprise that he was no longer coaching the school team, instead he was coaching netball. His failure to coach the school team was however not fatal because the team was under the expert guidance of another legend, Mudhara Felix Mbidzo. He was the Captain of the 1966 champions and therefore his football knowledge was immense. At the school he was now the bus driver and apart from coaching the team, he would drive them to matches on match day. This was total commitment to the development of the game. Mudhara Felix Mbidzo could have coached any team in the then Super League but he preferred to work with the school team and indeed the young players benefitted!

But dear reader, you might be wondering how this connection came about, Jawett Nechironga and Felix Mbidzo, teammates in 1966 now working at the same school that yours truly was attending? Well, there was a common denominator and the common denominator was none other than Father Arthur Davies, the Roman Catholic priest who was the Principal at the school. This is a man whose role in the development of Zimbabwe Football is rarely mentioned in present day football discussion. His contribution, however should never be underestimated. The man is an Unsung Hero! Well let me sing his name!

In 1951, he formed St. Pauls Musami Football club. By the 60's, the clergyman embarked on a mission to build a championship winning team in the then Rhodesia Football League. Over a period of time, he brought together a group of trainee teachers among them Jewatt Nechironga, Francis Tsatsa, some supporting staff like Felix Mbidzo and embarked on what became a remarkable journey of football conquest. He even tried to recruit the Mastermind himself George Shaya who was at Dynamos. He wanted to make him both a teacher and a football star, but Shaya was just too quiet to be a teacher, so the move fell through. With the remaining group of players, the good priest built a strong team which toppled the likes of Dynamos, Salisbury Callies and Mhangula Football Clubs to clinch the league in 1966. This was as remarkable feat because the team was based in rural Murehwa.

The topic of spreading the game of football into the rural areas and unearthing the abundant talent there is still a hot discussion among those who care for the development of the game. Well, the good priest walked the talk in 1966. His legacy still stands to this day, the first team from the rural areas to win the league and yes, he bestowed the area with a stadium, a stadium which still stands to day albeit in a dilapidated state. It is up to the sons and daughters of Murehwa to keep this legacy alive. They need to come together and help renovate this facility, it will be a worthy way to honour the now departed priest. He will smile from heaven if he sees this happening, The Father Davies Stadium, yes, that is some idea, but I leave that to the children of this great area.

After the demise of the St. Pauls team, Father Davies moved to Chishawasha Mission for a short spell before settling at St. Peters Kubatana where I found him working his magic. We were truly blessed to have such a luminary at our school. He had big plans for the school both sporting and academically.

On the education front, he had an open door policy. He believed in giving everyone an opportunity to develop. This is the reason why the school even offered places to students who had been expelled from other schools, the likes of Ticha whom I mentioned earlier. Some girls who had been impregnated and expelled often came to St. Peters to continue with their education. He also had a holistic education philosophy as he believed in training the mind, the hands and the heart. All kinds of courses were on offer and a technical college allowed those who wished to proceed with their mechanical courses to do so.

The good priest was ages ahead of his peers. On the sporting front, he wanted to start a football academy which would produce players for the European market and with time replicate the success story of St. Pauls Football Club. His vision was truly modern. The sporting facilities at the school were second to none and were a testimony of his commitment to football development.

Established football teams like Black Aces even begged to hold their training sessions at the school. We also had a lot of football kits and when other school teams used classrooms to change for matches, we had proper dressing rooms, showers and all. Those who were good enough to make it into the team were truly privileged and enjoyed their football. Father Davies truly believed in the power of sport and education to help the young people. He did encourage all sports, netball, volleyball, basketball, athletics but it is football which was his passion. What a leader he was!

Then politics came to the fore. There were grumblings from some teachers who accused Father Davies of wasting money on sporting activities at the expense of academic ones. The government moved in, appointed a new Headmaster and that signalled the death of the Academy project.

Our school team continued to do well winning in all the matches that we played. The team had the likes of Francis Nechironga, son to Jawett my music teacher, Darlington Choto and in later years we had John Mbidzo, son of Felix Mbidzo. Francis Nechironga was the star of the show. He was capable of scoring five goals in a match. A few records were broken by this team; like the time when they played a friendly match with the University of Zimbabwe. They beat them by thirty-three goals to three, that is some record scoreline which is embedded in the history of the school.

The old generation of Father Davies, Jawett Nechironga and Felix Mbidzo were our old heroes, but now new heroes were emerging. As earlier stated, our biggest star was Francis Nechironga. I remember when he flew to Lesotho with Caps United who were playing in the African Cup Winners in 1982.

This was the day the whole school came to a standstill. There was an official announcement at assembly and when he returned, the excitement blew our rooftops off. We had never seen the inside of a plane and so to have someone who had actually been inside a plane was nothing short of a miracle for us. Everyone wanted to touch him as if flying in the clouds had turned him into an extraterrestrial creature. "Did you actually use the toilet when you were up there?" one starry eyed young boy asked, clearly unable to envisage how that was possible. Francis Nechironga simply answered that with a smile. "What about a meal, did you have a meal?" someone wanted to know.

This was confirmed as true and good meal too the affable legend in the making added. "And yes, we took a nap when we were tired," added Francis. More gasps from the attentive audience, sleeping in the skies, wow, no one had ever heard of such a thing. The miracles of technology indeed! The plane had been demystified for us, we now had one among who could boast, "I went to the toilet in the plane." But now forty years later we now know better, many of us have been in planes countless times now.

While Francis was the well-known star, there was a publicity shy star whose football prowess only came to light by mistake. His name was Chris Chavhungama. Chris was a dribbling wizard but the whole school did not know about it. He preferred to keep his talent hidden from the school, something which even the the Bible teaches against in the parabale of the talents!

The teachers did not know, the sports master did not know and we as students were in the dark too. But one day, it came to light. How it happened was purely by accident. Chris who was already playing for BAT Ramblers, a mid table club in the Super league, played a blinder when he was introduced as a substitute. It was a night game and the following morning one of the teachers bought the newspaper. Chris was in the report because of his star performance. The teacher could not believe it and alerted the Head. The big announcement came at Assembly, "Chris Chavhungama, make sure you come for training today, you play for the school team first before you play for BAT Ramblers!" The whole school gasped, so we had a star at the school and we did not know!

The excitement levels shot through the roof. All the boys in the school descended on the training ground that afternoon. We wanted to see the new kid on the block, the new star born to the school. Chris did not disappoint, he showed the silky skills which he had kept away from our gaze for so long. What a privilege it was. We knew as cheering fans that our team would be unbeatable from that day onwards.

The reluctant star had come to the fore and the school team had an extra weapon to deploy against the hapless opposition in front of us. We played Mukai High school which had the likes of Mugove Munyorovi who later played for Dynamos and Mayor Eric who later played for Zimbabwe Saints, we beat them 8-0.
We played Highfields High School which had the likes of Stanley Chirambadare who later played for Dynamos, we beat them 5-0. No school team could withstand the massive talent at our disposal.

Another popular legend at this level was Weston Mvembe, we called him "Sekuru Jibha." Although he was not the most talented, his value came in him bringing a jovial atmosphere in the team. He loved slang words and often deployed them to encourage his teammates.

"Good going mwani!" was his statement of choice. He called everyone "Mwani" as in my man.

"Nice one younger!" He often said. "Ngatirove smatimbi boys!",his way of encouraging the lads to look smart. He loved socks up and shirts tucked in. He had a professional approach. I loved the company of Sekuru Jibha, what a character he was. He loved the game and he never shied from giving advice. I am sure if death had not cut short his life, he was going to be a very good coach.

Apart from football, the social and academic life was also exciting, and I made many friends, plenty of them. There was Petros Magada, I called him the mathematician, he tried to encourage me to like the subject but failed dismally. Maths was never my cup of tea, I harboured a phobia for the subject. Petros was also a keen marathon runner and participated in many of them. Then there was Samson Dodo, he prided himself as "a born and bred ghetto boy" or as we derogatively referred to him as "bornrukisheni" It was meant to put him down, but Sam would have none of it. Instead he turned on us and dismissed us as country bumpkins. Charles Maenzanise lived with a James Hadley Chase book by his side. Even during football matches, Chale would be busy with his novel, strange guy he was but he was a good friend.

I made progress with my schoolwork. As earlier stated, maths was a nightmare but English, history, shona and geography were my bread and butter. I was especially good at reading Shona and my teacher, Miss Nyamayaro relied on me to read to the whole class. If she was feeling lazy and did not want to attend lessons, which she often did, I would read the novel for the rest of the class.

My reading skills extended to English Literature and again I could be relied upon to give a good read for the class. My English language teacher, Mr. Mombeirere was a great guy but he was susceptible to the odd over indulgence of the brown bottle. Nursing a horrible hangover was no strange thing for him to do and when that happened, he often missed lessons. I would occupy the class by reading, Cry the Beloved Country by Allan Paton was my favourite, the class enjoyed it too. "There is a lovely road that runs from Ixopo into the hills. These hills are grass covered and rolling, and they are lovely beyond any singing of it", I read to the hushed attention of my classmates. We learnt a lot and we enjoyed it. My other favourite books were The Crucible, a play by Arthur

Miller and The Merchant of Venice by William Shakespeare.

Indeed, the school was good for me and to many other students who were given a second chance by Father Davies.Time flew and, before long, I sat for my Ordinary level examinations. I was confident of doing well and indeed when the results came, I had done well. I proceeded to A Level at Harare High School. As the saying goes, all is well that ends well. The label attached to St. Peters Kubatana High School did not affect me.

The school was not a graveyard of dreams as many suggested. Instead, It had enriched me from both an academic and football perspective. I had interacted with football royalty. The football elders I found at the school wetted my football appetite, my interest grew and deepened. Bambazonke? Far from from it! My earlier fears and apprehensions proved to be misplaced. I had a good time and I met the football heroes of 1966, the men who made St. Pauls Musami National Champions. What a priviledge!

Chapter 3
Hide and seek, A battle of Wills!

My father was a loving-man, but he was also very strict. He had a short fuse so to speak and it did not take much for him to blow his top. He was uncompromising on many things, his life principiles were cast in stone and he never wavered from his chosen position.

With him, there was little room for debate. It was his way or the highway! A question from him, an unsatisfactory answer and he deployed his weapon of choice, the belt which he would swiftly pull from his waist. It seemed to be there for that sole purpose! He disciplined us in the only way he knew how, subscribing as he did to the biblical exhortation "if you spare the rod, you spoil the child!" He took it literally; it was his way of showing his love for us by keeping us on the narrow and straight. He was a good father but his was tough love and his approach was old school. I do not blame him. He belonged to that generation of strict disciplinarians.

On most occasions, it was hide and seek with him. "Are you studying?" was the first question he asked whenever he came into our room. For him, it had to be books, books and more books. As boys we wanted to play, and we had to find a way to play since boys will be boys as the saying goes. So, we found a way to play football and yes to watch football. My young brother Clement was an accomplice in this, we were partners in crime.

We were a family of six initially in the four-roomed house that my father owned in Jerusalem in Highfield. My eldest brother Saul who had returned from a prison stint for attempting to join the liberation struggle, stayed with us briefly. He found a job with Southampton Insurance company and after marrying his young beautiful girlfriend, he quickly moved out to find his own place in Glen View. He loved Dynamos and still does. My eldest sister Violet had also returned from the war after spending five years in the bush decided that it was time to build a new nation by getting married to her wartime boyfriend. She too moved out, she knew nothing about football.

Then there was the one who left the breast for me as we say in our culture, Edward, he found a job soon after completing his 'O' levels with the Ministry of Education. He decided to move out and find his own place. He also loved Dynamos like my eldest brother and still does. And so, I remained with my young brother Clement, my young sister Ngaakudze but we were later to be joined by another brother Mandla, my new mother's son from an earlier marriage. We changed his name to its shona version Simba. Clement like me loved Caps United and to date the team is close to his heart. Ngaakudzwe, well she only listened to our endless football discussions, did she have a choice? Simba wanted to support Highlanders, but we made him a Caps United fan, he had to follow his elders.

Football consumed most of our time. It had to since we lived less than a kilometre away from Gwanzura Stadium, an arena of many football battles. The cheers from the fans in unison easily reached our residence so even without going to the stadium, our hearts and minds would be there. A further two hundred meters from Gwanzura Stadium were the iconic Zimbabwe Grounds, I call them the home of grassroots football in the suburb. As young boys, we literally lived our lives in these spacious four pitches. If we were not playing football, we were watching football during the weekend. There was the added luxury of also watching Caps United and Black Aces who used these pitches for their training sessions during

25

the course of the week. We never missed a training session and the love for football continued to grow.

We had to find a way to attend these training sessions, we had to find a way to evade the monitoring eye of our father.

"We are going to the library!" We said to our unsuspecting father as we wore our most innocent of faces.

"Well done, this is what I want to hear, make sure you concentrate," he would say with pride etched all over his beaming face.

If only he knew what was up our sleeves! We did not wait for him to question our newly found zeal for the reading room. Picking up a few books, we would disappear towards Highfield Community Library. However, Highfield Community library was only a detour. The real destination was the legendary Zimbabwe grounds. For the next two or three hours, our books would be in the library while we were busy cheering the silky skills of Shambo, the lethal finishing of Shacky Tauro, the power of Friday Phiri, the midfield mastery of Stanford Mtizwa and the graceful movement and the cheeky smile of Stanley Ndunduma and all the other Caps United players going through their paces. This was heaven on earth and our love for this team was cemented. For over two or three years, we never missed a Caps United training session at the Zimbabwe grounds. Father never found out about our journey into football fandom under the guise of spending time in the library. I am glad he never did, I shudder to think what would have happened!

Indeed, in all things football related, it was hide and seek with father. Sunday was especially difficult for us. Father expected us to be in church the whole day and yet Gwanzura Stadium would be beckoning too. Our fancifully named church, The Church of God of Prophecy under the leadership of Bishop Kenneth Nyamhuka made Sunday a truly worshipping day. There was no room for anything else with worship services starting at ten in the morning and ending at five oclock! For the Elders it was ok, as they listened attentively to sermons of hell, damnation and salvation. They would sing, worship and cry tears of repentance as they tried to make peace with God. But for the young it was a nightmare. How could one spend close to nine hours in church? So we had to find a way and after much scratching of heads, we came up with a plan.

At around two o'clock before the afternoon service commenced, we used to ask father for offering money. Indeed the Holy book encourages us not to appear before the good Lord empty handed! Father was aware of this so he emptied the last coins in his wallet into our grateful palms! We took the coins, fully aware that they would not find their way into the offering basket. For us we knew we had lulled father into a false sense of security. We knew that having seen us at two o'clock, he would not question our being in church the whole afternoon. We sat right at the back next to the exit and It was easy for us to just slip out of church unnoticed and off to Gwanzura Stadium we went.

After watching the match, we rushed home and to cover our tracks we found out the message of the day from our young sister Ngaakudzwe. She knew our love for football and she would gladly share the message. By the time father came to us to discuss the message, we were ready.

"Yes, what an inspiring message, we enjoyed it!" we said, exchanging some knowing smiles. Father would leave us in peace, satisfied that the word was not falling on rocky ground, that it was germinating in our hearts. If only he knew that, we had used the offering money to buy some ice creams as we watched the match! All hell would have broken loose.

In Highfield, all the boys played football in the streets. I understand the youth of today have other interests but for us it was football, football and more football. We were also obsessed with staying fit, "stamina" we used to call it. We kept line ups of soccer teams like Dynamos, Caps United, Rio Tinto among others. Rio Tinto always fascinated us, the players looked super fit, their physical built was impressive. We knew that their coach John Rugg was a firm believer in physical fitness and used to put them through some gruelling runs which built their physic or "stamina" as we called it. Seeing players like Ephert Lungu, Joseph Zulu, Robert Godoka and company running onto the pitch at Gwanzura left us awe struck. They looked like super human beings. Another super fit group of players were the Hwange players like Nyaro Mumba, Benson Soko, Chingumbe Masuku and these inspired us to build our fitness.

Often, we embarked on road runs and we also spent time in Gwanzura Stadium running up and down the terraces. We had a special name for it, "kuMasteps", it was a rite of passage. Every young boy worth his salt who lived in Highfield went through this process. There were some elders in the hood, fitness fanatics themselves like Bla Jones and Bla Watson who used to motivate us.

We all wanted to look like Ephert Lungu, David Mwanza or Nyaro Mumba, a special specimen of footballers who looked invincible. We never managed to reach those levels, but we tried our best and indeed we looked good. We often showed off our physique by wearing tight shorts to expose the well-built thighs. We never missed a chance to show off our developing muscles. It was all fun!

Money games also helped to develop our love for the sport. These were both a test of football skills and bravery. It was one thing to put the money down for a bet, play the game and win, but claiming the money was the biggest test. You had to be prepared to fight for the money especially if it was against Malaga's team from Engineering.

Yes, many in the Zimbabwe Grounds where we used to meet for the money games feared Malaga. He was not physically imposing but somehow he managed to strike fear in the hearts of many. If therefore you played a game with his team, chances were that win or lose, the difference was the same. Getting the money from Malaga and his team was as impossible as trying to ride on the back of a lion. Often enough we refused to play with his team but when he chose to, he could be charming and persuade us to agree. But at the end of the match, if Malaga 's team lost, the money still stayed with Malaga's team. He was indeed some character and there were many like him. In the end we simply walked away or on occasion fought for our money but that was rare. On most occassions we decided to keep the peace.

This arena was the home of grassroots football in the 1980s, the Zimbabwe grounds also provided free entertainment for most Highfield residents especially the men and the boys. Of course the women and girls came too but this was usually to sell foodstuffs such as groundnuts, boiled eggs and maize cobs. Indeed, roaring business was conducted by these ingenious women and girls who never missed an opportunity to make an extra dollar.

Meanwhile, the men were busy watching football and some great football was dished out every weekend at these iconic grounds. There were so many teams which went pound for pound against each other on these four pitches. The entertainment lasted almost the whole day. The need to refuel and eat something was paramount and so the women's business came in handy.

Many teams plied their trade in the Zimbabwe Grounds. Some were company teams such as Saltrama

Plastics, Eversharp, Rothmans, Cafenol, Ferco among others. It is evident from the list that our industrial base as a nation was still very firm, production levels were quite high and companies could afford to sponsor teams. The added advantage for most players was the employment which these companies offered albeit being low skilled work.

Apart from the company owned teams, there were some community owned teams like Chipinge United, Lusaka Hotspurs and Murehwa Football Club. Many young players started their careers with these teams, players such as Nyasha Kanogoiwa, Emmanuel Nyahuma, Silver Chigwenje, Shadreck Dzvairo, Itai Kapini, Allen Mapila who went on to play for top teams like Dynamos and Black Aces. These players benefitted from having so many teams around to enhance their football skills. Even the not so talented players could find teams, there was no shortage of teams to join. Sometimes teams would struggle for players especially on Sunday for the early 8 o'clock kickoffs. It was easy to discern why, hangover!

Many players indeed struggled to wake up after a heavy Saturday night. Why the League organisers insisted on these early morning fixtures, only God knows. Many teams were often desperate and sometimes they had to pick players from the early bird fans, "Unogona bhora here mupfanha?", was the desperate question. "Can you play young man?", if the answer was yes, it was game time.

While the Sunday morning matches might have looked a bit shambolic, it does not mean that the players were poor. In fact, there were some really good players. Let me talk about a few, legends of the local game, very good players who were happy to just play in this league even though a higher calling was possible.

There was Bla Chale, I never got to know his full name. He played for Chipinge United and the man was a goal getter par excellence. He was good with both feet and was lethal in the air. He never ended a match without getting a goal and often, he bagged two or three. Bla Chale was capable of scoring thirty to forty goals per season, his talent deserved a better league, but he never bothered to move.

There was Gake, another one who used a nickname and played for Lusaka Hotspurs. He was a midfield enforcer whose ability to win the ball and pass it was a marvel to watch. He was brave too but one day his bravery cost him dearly. A shot was hit with venom, Gake decided to control it with his chest. But the shot was too hard, it knocked him out and he lost control of his bowels. By the time the first aid was administered which usually involved the pouring water and more water on his prostrate body, Gake woke up to find his shorts covered with poo. It is a story which the people of Highfield still talk about, some forty years later. This does not take away from his legendary status, it actually enhances it. These things happen in the thick of battle!

We had Mashaka who played for Saltrama, the plastic recycling company. We called him Bla Shaks and what a defender he was. He was renowned for his bone crushing tackles, strikers feared him. One tackle from him could signal the end of the match. He took no prisoners, he played to win, and he tackled to instil fear in strikers. The only other player who matched him when it came to tackles was China a defender for Lusaka Hotpurs. His father the Bishop of my father's church, The Church of God of Prophecy, had given him the name Signs, but we called him China because of his karate like tackles which often left opponents writhing with pain on the surface. Seeing China on the pitch, you could never imagine that he was the son of such an esteemed Bishop. For him, football was not the beautiful game, it was a game in which he deployed all the dark arts, and these were epitomised in his flying tackles.

31

There are others who still make me misty eyed as I go down memory. George, an accomplished midfielder, we called him Tigana after the great French midfield maestro. He was some player, ball control, an eye for a pass and shooting from a distance, he had it all in the locker. He was popular with the fans and every time he was on the pitch, he never disappointed. Then there was Shambo, another one who used a moniker. He had adopted the great Joel Shambo's name and although he fell far short of the great maestro's qualities, he was not a bad midfielder. I am sure if he had pushed himself, he could have played in the super league.

And yes, I played too for Cairns United which was sponsored by a car manufacturing company and contributed to the entertainement. My young brother Clement was even better and he captained the teams that he played for. I am sure with better encouragement he could have played in the then Super League. Indeed, the Zimbabwe Grounds were the home of grassroots football in our suburb. We watched games from morning to mid afternoon on Saturday and once these games had finished, we went to Gwanzura Stadium to watch the big boys. It was all fun and it kept us from mischief.

It is such a shame that no improvements have been made to these iconic grounds. If the Council pays attention to recreation grounds, the Zimbabwe grounds can be turned into centres of excellence for junior football and other sports. Indeed, it is a truth universally accepted that when young people are engaged in sports, they will stay away from mischief. The scourge of drugs and alcoholism can be minimised among the young. Sport is a panacea for many ills.

My father did not know it then, but he had a lot to thank the Zimbabwe Grounds for, they kept us safe. Ofcourse as young boys we had our naughty moments, we even tried the occasional weed smoking, but it did not take over our lives. We were too busy playing football to descend into drug addiction.

I also remember my football experience at Harare High School, a school that I joined for my A-level studies. By this time, I was physically fully developed, and I could hold my own in the first team. Our school team had many good players and most of them went on to play top flight football. Our Captain, Tendai Chapo played for Black Mambas. Others like Stanley Chimwanza and Jomo Takawira were with Black Rhinos while Louis Sande played for Fire Batteries. Football at High school also introduced me to the world of love.

I must admit, I was a late entry to all things romantic. One day after a match against Mabvuku High School, we boarded the school bus as usual. I was sitting on my own until one young girl came and said "Hie, my name is Beauty, I know you, I like how you play football!" Self praise has no recommendation, but Beauty was right, I was a good defender with immaculate ball control skills. I preferred to pass the ball from the back rather than just boot it upfield. A modern defender so to speak, that was what I was way back in 1986.

I did not know how to respond to Beauty, my mouth was dry, I simply nodded my head and thanked her for the compliment. Dear reader, this journey suddenly became very long, and we travelled it in silence all the way from Mabvuku to Mbare. I could not wait to get off the bus. I was sweating profusely! But the biggest surprise for me came the following Monday. The daring Beauty passed a note to my best friend Francis Garaba, "how was your weekend, I missed you!" it read.

Oh my God, this was love and I felt it for the first time. Football had opened a door that I did not know existed, a glimpse into the world of love. From then on, whenever I played football for the school, it had taken on a new significance. I was doing it for the school but also to impress Beauty. It eventually ended but it was fun while it lasted! I hope my wife Tendai who is editing this story will allow this episode to go through, "Kuyaruka kwevakomana" as we say, "boys growing up!"

From my father I learnt many things: love, respect, hard work; he always preached about unity but about football, I learnt nothing. It was hide and seek with him to play football. It was hide and seek with him to watch football. However, together with my brother Clement, we found a way to enjoy football without landing ourselves into hot soup. I have a rich football experience from my youth, an experience I nurtured by finding a way to evade the eagle eyes of my father.

We had to make up stories, we dumped books in the library to watch Caps United train, we scaled over the wall at Gwanzura Stadium, "Kupoya", we had good days with Mudhara Hunha the caretaker and bad ones too, running battles with the Fawcett Security guards who manned the gates, even with the police. We lied about being in church, all for the love of the game! Indeed, once the football bug had caught us, there was no going back. The bug is still there even as I write this chapter, the setting has now changed, but not the love is undiluted!

Chapter 4
The golden generation: A missed opportunity!

Doctor Rinozivei Zhuwarara was a great teacher! He left a permanent impression on my young mind. At the University of Zimbabwe, I interacted with many lecturers, but none had quite the same impact on me like the man with the legendary name...Rinozivei. I love indigenous names, they are always loaded with meaning and the good doctor's name was loaded, why that name? What inspired his parents to give him that name? but I digress!

When Lucifer Mandengu in Waiting for the Rain by the legendary writer, Charles Mungoshi, declared, "My name is Lucifer Mandengu. I was born here against my will, it was a biological and geographical error...if I go away, I will not come back..." Dr Rinozivei was livid! He called him the fallen angel, a man with no identity, a man totally alienated from his roots, a man doomed! He condemned him for rejecting his family, people, culture, for rejecting the very essence of his being. With such betrayal, Dr. Rinozivei had no sympathy and he persuaded us to agree with him. Even as we gathered with my friends Francis Garaba, Fortune Mzondo, Lovemore Taruza, Tonderayi Chanakira and Tichaona "Deuchmark" Zinhumwe at the iconic Students Union bar, bottles of castle and lion lager occupying most of the space on the table, the air thick with Kingsgate and Madison tobacco toasted fumes, we joined in the condemnation of Lucifer. We swore that we would never be like Lucifer Mandegu and that we were true sons of the soil!

But allow me dear reader to speculate about the golden legends of our football, legends I can rightly say were victims of a geographical error to borrow from

Lucifer 's speech or rather victims of history. Could they have played at a higher level for the likes of Manchester United, Arsenal, Liverpool, Real Madrid or Barcelona had they been born in territories other that the geographical location that destiny placed them in.

Could they have reached the very top had history been kinder? Without endorsing Lucifer Mandengu's self hate, I posit that we had many such legends whose talents deserved world exhibition. Historical realities stopped some, they were victims of an unjust political situation which invited sporting sanctions. The racist white minority government made it difficult for other progressive nations to establish sporting links with the country. The sporting isolation took a toll on the careers of many talented footballers. For some, soon after independence, the lack of exposure coupled with the lack of agents who had a better understanding of the workings of world football, scuppered many talents. In the end we as local fans were the beneficiaries, but I keep wondering how far these legends could have gone. Consider this, Eusebio from dusty Lourenco Marques, Mozambique departed for Portugal, he became a global star. I wonder what George "Mastermind" Shaya could have done if the same opportunity had opened for him. Interesting thoughts but let us explore this in detail.

Before Rhodesia became Zimbabwe in 1980, sporting sanctions were in place due to the racist policies of the Ian Smith led white supremacist government. The whole world did not want anything to do with Rhodesia on the sporting front. This I am afraid affected the careers of many stars who could have travelled abroad to play for the world's best teams. There are two who escaped these debilitating sanctions like bustling striker Freddy" Mark Makwesha" Mkwesha who went to Portugal to play for Sporting De Braga in 1966 and Bruce "Jungleman" Grobbelaar who went to Canada in 1979 to play for

Vancouver Whitecaps before becoming one of the greatest goalkeepers in the world with Liverpool a team he joined in 1981.

Freddy Mkwesha who many consider to be the deadliest finisher the country has ever produced, spent many years in Portugal where he rubbed shoulders with the black diamond Eusebio of Mozambique who was now playing for Benfica on the battlefield. Bruce on the other hand who established himself as the crown Prince of goalkeepers with his eccentric style, went on to win six titles, three FA Cups, three league Cups and one European cup, a remarkable achievement in his long career with Liverpool. But there are many who stayed behind in the stifling atmosphere of racist Rhodesia. They were denied the opportunity to exhibit their skills on the international arena, they were victims of an unfortunate historical epoch, a geographical error.

The first who comes to mind is George "Mastermind" Shaya, regarded by many as the greatest footballer to emerge from the country. The football elders whom I talk with will put their last dollar on a bet that Shaya could have walked into any dressing room in Europe and nailed a first team place. He was the complete player, football genius personified who made Dynamos Football Club one of the most feared teams in the country and the most supported.

Some claim that because of his scintillating displays, million of supporters joined the Glamour Boys Dynamos fan base. Shaya dominated the Zimbabwe football terrain, winning the coveted Soccer Star of the Year award a record five times in 1969,1972,1975,1976 and 1977. This was no mean feat if one considers the quality of players who were in the league then. There are claims which I could not verify that he was offered trials in Portugal. Maybe it was a brief stint and did not allow him to show his class. What I can say without doubt is that his talent deserved a world stage, a stage occupied by the likes of Eusebio the Mozambique born "Black Diamond". "The Mastermind" was the real deal. Other legends of this era included Tendai Chieza, Joseph Zulu, Ebson "Sugar" Muguyo, Peter "Thunderboots" Nyama who once scored sixty-two goals in 1971, Matthew Mwale, Posani Sibanda, Shadreck Ngwenya, Brendan Galloway, Kevin Sheridan, Topsy Robertson, Bill Sherman to mention a few. These were all top players who with enough exposure to the world arena could have held their own.

Joseph Zulu of Rio Tinto holds the record for the soccer star of the year finalist selection, he was among the finalists ten times. Zulu was offered a chance to join Manchester United in 1978. He had been offered the chance of a one-month trial by the Red Devils, but the Rio Tinto management put spanners in the move.

"What hurts more is that Gary Bailey who I was supposed to accompany on the trip went on to become a good goalkeeper for Manchester United, my club said if I go, the club will go down. I was playing unbelievable football, John Rugg always asked me, how did you do that, if I had gone my family was going to be well off. The team was selfish, I was so hurt, I did not train for a month," Joseph said in an interview with the Herald newspaper. He is still bitter about the aborted move. The club also scuppered moves to Greece and Cameroon. What a blow it was for Zulu, a football great whose talents demanded a higher profile.

I am also tempted to ask how does a striker score sixty-two goals in one season and not be entered into the Guinness book of records? Yet this was the feat that Peter "Thunderboots" Nyama achieved in his football career. His nickname says it all, what a finisher he was! The man deserved to play at a higher level.He deserved a world audience.

There were great midfielders too talents who deserved a higher calling. Shaw "Kojak" Handriade, was a super fit midfield workhorse who specialised in long range drives, "grass cutters" as they were called. Then there was William Sibanda, he was what we now call a "box to box midfielder" in modern football parlance. For the modern reader, think about Patrick Viera at his peak with Arsenal and you have a picture of William Sibanda in the 1970's. He was clearly a talent ahead of his time and could have been comfortable in the top European leagues. I did not watch most of these legends but from the discussion I have had with many elders of the game, I am told that they deserved a higher stage to exhibit their skills.

My heart also goes out to those legends whom I watched soon after independence. Yes, sanctions were immediately lifted soon after independence but again lack of exposure and proactive agents who could promote our players put paid to any moves that might have happened. As earlier stated I fell in love with the Caps United team of the 1980's. In that magical team there were football magicians like Joel Shambo, Stanley Ndunduma, Shacky Tauro, Stix Mtizwa and Friday Phiri whose abilities could have taken them to the best leagues in the world.

There were many good teams in our league aptly named the Super League and each team boasted at least four great players, capable of mixing it up with the best at the world stage. My first love, Caps United had Shacky Tauro, a master goal scorer. He was a finisher, a man capable of scoring twenty-five plus goals in a season. Nothing gave him more joy than to score goals, he was a born predator, a goal machine and fans recognised this by giving him the nickname "Mr Goals"

I have no doubt that if he had moved abroad in his prime, the world would still be talking about this goal scorer par excellence. While Shacky was a goal machine, it does not mean that he had it all his way, for indeed there were some hot shots too who gave him a run for his money. The babyfaced assassin, Wonder Chaka of Gweru United was one of them and so was Maronga Nyangela nicknamed "The Bomber" for his venomous shots. I have never seen a player who hit the ball so hard. There was also George Rollo who once tore the nets with a fierce shot during one match at Rufaro. He declared "Tell them that TNT is back!". That was his nickname, TNT. Indeed, he was like dynamite. He could explode. There were many more like Gift "Ghetto" Mpariwa who lived to score goals, Charles "Chola" Chirwa who had a lethal left foot. These were top strikers who deserved the highest stage to exhibit those God given talents.

Then came Moses "Razorman "Chunga who announced himself with a bang by scoring 46 goals in one season in 1986. Moses Chunga was capable of performing miracles on the pitch. No situation was too hard for "Moze" as his legion of fans called him, he created goals out of nowhere. Apart from the goals, he mesmerised defences with his dribbling skills and like George Shaya before him, I think he helped to grow the Dynamos support base. A fan, Cliff Mparutsa had this to say about him.

"Moses Chunga was the real deal during his era. He redefined the way football was played. Every child wanted to be like Moze. His arrogance on and off the pitch divided the opinion of fans. One thing for certain, no one could ignore him. His name is up there with the best in Zimbabwe football history." Although Moses later moved to the Belgium league, I think he deserved to play in the much stronger leagues like Germany, Italy or England.

There were great midfielders whose midfield artistry also demanded a higher stage. Stanford "Stix" Mtizwa, the man who made the chest control his trademark, is one of them. In world football we have the Cruyf turn as perfected by Johan Cruyff the Netherlands football genius and the Panenka penalty which was introduced to the football world by Antonin Panenka the Czech star. Well, I can state without doubt that in the Zimbabwe football narrative, the chest control can rightfully be called the "Mtizwa control". No one controlled the ball better with his chest than Stike or " Mwaluvha" as his peers called him. His touch was so deft that one day the referee stopped the match to check if the ball still had pressure. That is how comfortable Mtizwa was with the ball on his chest.

Mtizwa was also a great dribbler and a master of the defence splitting passes. He could have moved to Belgium but his club, military outfit Black Rhinos stopped the move. "I was heartbroken, I still have the contract that I was supposed to sign, I am still bitter", he recently said. His midfield partner at Caps United, before he moved to Rhinos was Joel Shambo, so good the fans nicknamed him "The Headmaster" or "Mwalimu." Handsome and ever smiling, the legend was midfield mastery personified. He was a leader on and off the pitch and made many fall in love with football. I think he deserved a higher league.

If we add to the mix, Archford Chimutanda, the master of ball control and great passes, the list becomes longer. He was another midfield genius. None controlled the ball better than Archford, none passed it better than "Chehuche". But Archie was a flawed genius, he often skipped training and maybe because of that, he was never going to make it to the world stage.

David "Chikwama" Mwanza, was a workaholic and he was often the first name on the team sheet for his clubs and the National team. Mwanza was blessed with all the qualities that are needed in a midfielder. He had the energy to run up and down the park, he had the skills to go past defenders and he was blessed with a powerful shot. On many occasions, Chikwama as he was nicknamed popped in to score a thunderbolt from a distance. I think because of his strength, he would have fitted in well into any

English team. Most European teams in the 80's valued hard work and discipline and these Chikwama had in abundance. What an all-round midfielder he was, I am convinced that he could have made it to the very top.

There was the stylish Willard "Mahwi" Khumalo, a great midfielder who also loved to entertain the fans. Like Mwanza, Mahwii as we called him was a complete midfielder, ball control, understanding of space and the eye for a good pass. He made it easy for the strikers giving them some gift-wrapped passes. I have no doubt in my mind that the very top was his destiny in the game. He later moved but it was rather late, if he had moved in his early twenties, his impact would have been more. Robert Godoka, Max Tshuma, David Mandigora, Stanley "Sinyo" Ndunduma, David Muchineripi, Titus Majola were capable of mixing it with any of the world's greatest stars.

Another great midfielder who emerged in the 80's was Memory Mucherahowa. On many occasions, he was linked with a move abroad but his team, Dynamos often scuppered the moves. With better representation, his talent was crying out for a bigger league but unfortunately it never happened. The list of good midfielders cannot be listed on one page but the ones I have mentioned stood a great chance of making it in Europe.

The art of defending is often underestimated but before injury cut his career short, Sunday Marimo was nicknamed "Never on Sunday". Be it at Gwanzura Stadium, Rufaro Stadium, Cam and Motor Stadium or Barbourfileds, on any Sunday afternoon, it was difficult to go past Sunday Marimo. He is a man who could have felt at home in any defensive line up in the world. Then there was Ephraim Chawanda, although he later played briefly in Europe, that was at a lower level. His talent deserved a bigger stage, so did that of Francis Shonhayi. What about Mercedes Sibanda, the man known by fans as Rambo? He had the heart of lion and he indeed played like a lion. Ephert

42

Lungu was strong and unbeatable, Douglas "British" Mloyi was no nonsense, James Takawada was intelligent and reliable, so was the stylish John Mbidzo, Oliver Kateya was known for his overlapping runs which created so many opportunities for his strikers. Alexander Maseko was known as the "Cool Ruler" because he never panicked under pressure. I dare say all these defenders were capable of mixing it up with the very best.

In the goalkeeping department, Zimbabwe was well represented by the "Jungleman" Bruce Grobelaar who reached dizzy heights with Liverpool but there are those who were content to ply their trade on the local scene. The country had talent galore in this area, legends such as Posani Sibanda, Frank Mkanga, Musa Muzanenhamo and Mathew Mwale who were all capable of playing for the world's greatest teams. Another one was Japhet Mparutsa, a man nicknamed "Short Cat" for his lack of vertical elevation, but what an acrobatic goalkeeper he was. For over a decade, Japhet was the top goalie among the many talented goalkeepers in Zimbabwe.

"The Short Cat," as his legions of fans called him, is a man who defied the odds. He was short, which is usually a negative for a goalkeeper, but he compensated this with the agility and the acrobatics which gave rise to that moniker, "Short Cat." The fact that he won the soccer star of the year as a mere nineteen-year old says a lot about his goalkeeping prowess. He was the first goalkeeper to achieve this feat in 1982 in the Zimbabwe football fraternity. He deserved a chance in the football arenas of Europe.

This decade also produced Brenna Msiska who went on to spend close to two decades as a topflight goalkeeper in Zimbabwe. At his peak, I think he could have cut it among the best. The same can be said about Peter Fanwell nicknamed "Chops", what a goalkeeper he was. He was blessed with both height and amazing agility. I have faith that if the opportunity had arisen in those early years of his career, he could have played abroad.

It will be amiss to forget those who kept us on the edge of our seats in the terraces, the dribbling wizards. I will dedicate a chapter to these wizards but allow me to mention only one who gave defenders sleepless nights. Maxmillion Ndlovu or "Boy," as the fans knew him. The man had bags of tricks which made it a nightmare for any defenders he faced. Rumour has it that he dribbled many defenders into retirement.

I watched him in one match against Caps United, wow, it was a torrid time for giant left back Size Torindo. "Boy", a diminutive genius almost made a mockery of the legendary defender's claims to be a Super League defender. He dribbled him, he nutmegged him, he outran him, it was a dribbling master class. By the end of the match, the fans rose to salute a football artist, they had witnessed something special. I can declare without a shadow of doubt that the man could have walked into any European club dressing room and felt at home. We talk about Sir Stanley Mathews as the wizard of the wing, well Boy Ndlovu could have given him a run for his money had it not been for his geographical location.

Indeed, these were special players and for me it was also the golden age of Zimbabwe football. The age that made me fall in love with Zimbabwean football. There were many great teams and there were many great players. In later years we had several players who managed to play abroad. They had agents who were able to find teams for them abroad.

They had the talent to make an impact on the foreign soil. Players like Peter Ndlovu, Benjamin Maruwari, Cephas Chimedza, Harrington Shereni, Agent Sawu and currently Marvellous Nakamba and Tino Kadewere, who went to Europe. They represented us well, but this representation could have come much earlier had historical circumstances been different. Unfortunately, the golden generation of players never had their chance.

Yes, this was a golden age, an age when football superstars used grace our pitches. What an age it was to be alive. The fans were enthused but did these legends deserve a higher platform to exhibit those talents had the circumstances of history and their geographical location been different? I dare to say yes and I know my esteemed lecturer Dr. Rinoziwei will agree with me if he reads this!

Chapter 5
The Nicknames we gave them

"Daidzaivamwe!" I consider this as the mother of all football nicknames in Zimbabwe. It is a moniker which can be interpreted on two levels, "Daidzaivamwe" as in call everyone so they can see the amazing skills or "Daidzivamwe" when the defender might be calling others to come and help because the legend was difficult to stop in one versas one situations!" Whichever way one chooses to view the nickname, it remains one of the most interesting, ever given to a football player in our country.

The man who carried it was worth the beauty of the nickname and the effort put into creating it. Nkulumo Donga, what a player he was! I will talk about him in more detail because in this chapter of my football journey, I want to explore the nicknames which we gave our football stars. They range from the creative to the simply uncharitable. Players love them, players also hate them, but the truth is no Zimbabwe football narrative can be complete without an exploration of this interesting topic, nicknames!

Even as we played football in the dusty streets or at the Zimbabwe grounds, we gave each other nicknames. Often, we adopted the names of the good players in the league. My friends called me "Chivhima" after the Rio Dairiboard defender of the early 80's, Jonathan Chivhima who took no prisoners when getting into a tackle. He often took the man and the ball. I did not play like that, but I found myself burdened with this nickname. Many boys adopted names of their heroes like Shambo, Godoka or Shortcat in an attempt to emulate these stars.

One of the boys in our team had the habit of adopting a new nickname every week. If it was Stix Mtizwa who had played well on that weekend, Kaguda would spend the whole week calling himself Stix Mtizwa. If it was Madinda Ndlovu, he would call himself Madinda or Khatazile. He would spend the whole match praising himself calling out the name which would have caught his fancy that week. He was a funny guy, Kaguda, "Icho Kaguda, icho Stike, icho Madinda, chakaipa! There goes Madinda, there goes Stike, he is bad news", he would engage in a running commentary of himself, he encouraged and praised himself as he played. What a great character, Kaguda was popular with all the boys at the playground. Everyone wanted Kaguda to be around because he always raised the morale. It was all good fun!

Then there was a midfield star whose failure to play top flight football will forever be a mystery, he was good. We nicknamed called him "Tigana", his real name was George. He was a box to box midfielder just like the former France great, Jean Tigana so Tigana was an apt nickname. What a shame that he did not reach the zenith of his football career.

And yes, those legends whom we spend so much time trying to emulate had their nicknames too. The nicknames often denoted the abilities of the players but sometimes they simply captured their personalities. For example, Gift Mpariwa was a prolific goal scorer who banged in goals with aplomb.

Many stories circulated about how his goal scoring exploits were motivated by one thing, the bonuses which came with a win. He loved the money and for him football was for the cash that came after the win. His love of money gave rise to the nickname "Muduso" which is township slang for money. He was also known as "Ghetto" which was an acknowledgement of his ghetto background, the tough ghetto of Mufakose where he grew up. Muduso gobbled up all the scoring chances that came his way, he knew that by scoring and by winning football matches, the winning bonuses were guaranteed.

There was George Shaya, a football genius who won the Soccer Star of the year award a record five times, (1969, 1972, 1975, 1976 and 1977), he was nicknamed "Mastermind". This was in recognition of his abilities as a footballer, a man who always engaged his brain when on the pitch. The man had everything in the locker, ball control, an eye for the pass, dribbling, scoring ability and the quality which often separates the boys from the men, a football brain.

Tales are told of how George would stand by the touchline, in deep thought figuring out how to change a game. After a few minutes of reflection, he would then rejoin the action and from that moment onwards, the game changed. With the ball at his feet, defenders were in trouble. He dazzled with his endless tricks keeping the fans at the edge of their seats. For close to a decade from 1969, Shaya was the king in the Zimbabwean football fraternity. There were many great players during this era, but he was generally accepted as the best and for that the nickname "Mastermind" was no exaggeration.

The two men who are often mentioned in the same sentence with Shaya in terms of football greatness, Moses Chunga and Peter Ndlovu also had some interesting nicknames. Many fans still argue that Moses Chunga was almost as good as George Shaya, it is a debate which divides opinion. What cannot be disputed is that Moses was a great player whose talent made him a Dynamos favourite, earning him a professional contract in Belgium.The Dynamos faithful were quick to recognise his football talents and for that they gave him the nickname "Razorman". Let me explain the "Razorman" nickname in greater detail.

In 1983, Moses Chunga burst on to the local football scene and took the breath of many fans away with his dazzling skills. At about the same time, Lever Brothers, the flagship household goods producing company, launched a new shaving product and the man to advertise it was known as The Razorman. No situation was beyond this fictional hero all because he was always clean-shaven. He solved many difficult situations and was presented as a people's hero. Moses Chunga was the same; no football situation was beyond his unbelievable talents. If Dynamos were struggling, Moses often came to the rescue and defences parted before him like the Red Sea did for the biblical Moses!

For Dynamos, with Moses leading the line, any football hurdle was easily overcome. He was indeed a miracle worker for Dembare. He became a fans favourite and hero so the nickname "Razorman" resonated with the fans and his fame spread far and wide." Razorman" became the man for all occasions, a man who never let his followers down, a man who solved the most difficult of football situations.

There are others in the Zimbabwe football fraternity who argue the case for Peter Ndlovu as one of the best footballers to emerge from the country. Again, it is a debate which divides opinion, but the consensus is there that Peter was a great player.Peter burst onto the local scene in 1988, blowing defenders away with his pace, dribbling skills and audacious finishes. The fans were excited; they thronged the stadiums to watch the baby-faced star deliver stellar performances every weekend. He did not stay long at his parent club Highlanders because his immense talents attracted the attention of Coventry City in the English First Division, a club he duly joined in 1991. However, before he left, his jaw-dropping skills and performances had made the creative fans come up with one of the best nicknames to match a great footballer. They called him "Nsunkusonke" – a Ndebele word which means "Everyday Wonder." The nickname captured who Peter was – an everyday wonder. He delivered wonderful performances in every match. Peter Ndlovu on song was unstoppable. He was a gift from God!

Other stars had more than one nickname given to them. We called Joel Shambo "The Headmaster" or alternatively" Mwalimu". Shambo illuminated the football pitch with his abundant football skills which made fans come to the stadium in droves. He was a complete midfielder. He had it all – exquisite ball skills, a work ethic, leadership and, yes, the looks to melt even a heart of stone. During one match against perennial rivals Dynamos, Joel Shambo produced a midfield master class creating five goals in a seven-nil drubbing of the old foe. Sam Marisa, the then Herald newspaper editor wrote, "The man who did the damage for Dynamos was none other than Joel Shambo, the man they call the Headmaster. Shambo was in such imperious form that he reduced the Dynamos midfield players to his students."

Marisa could not have captured it any better. On this day, Shambo destroyed Dynamos. He became a cult hero among the Caps United faithful. This was not a one off. Indeed "The Headmaster" was capable of such performances every weekend. His nickname "Mwalimu" is Swahili for teacher, again denoting his football abilities. Legendary Tanzanian President, a political thinker of note, was known simply as Mwalimu. Well Joel Shambo was also a Mwalimu – a teacher as well as a leader on the football pitch!

Another legend with several nicknames was Oliver Kateya known as "The Flying Saucer" For his speed down the wings as a left back and "Monitoring Force" for his abilities to keep wingers in his "pocket" to use a football metaphor. "Monitoring Force" will need a bit of explanation because it has historical significance. During the transition from Rhodesia to Zimbabwe in 1979, a monitoring force was put in place to maintain the peace and to keep the former warring parties apart. The man who led the country at this pivotal historical epoch was British Governor, Lord Soames.

The Monitoring force was composed of British soldiers. It secured the peace to allow for a peaceful election. Our creative fans took it upon themselves to give this name to one of their own, so Oliver Kateya became "The Monitoring Force." Indeed, he kept an eagle eye on the wingers who might have caused problems for his team Dynamos.

At roughly the same time, Mark Watson, a striker for Highlanders was also banging in the goals for his team. Since he was white, the fans were quick, they called him "Lord Soames." So out of this historical epoch, we now had "The Monitoring Force" and "Lord Soames" in our football narrative. Dynamos had another great player, Edward Katsvere, we called him "Madhobha" or "Twinkletoes" for his dribbling wizadry. What a player, a crowd favourite even for rival supporters. He often gave defenders a torrid time with his dazzling footwork.

Then there was Daidzaivamwe. Oh my God! What a nickname befitting a dribbling wizard of note, Nkulumo Donga of Chapungu Football Club. As earlier intimated in my introduction, for the uninitiated, Daidzaivamwe which can be literally translated to "Please call others" was a clarion call to call others to come and witness the footwork of this genius. It was also a clarion call from defenders to say, "Please come and help I cannot handle this on my own." Indeed, to miss a match that Nkulumo played was to miss a spectacle so fans heeded the call to come and watch. The defenders who faced Nkulumo every weekend had to double up on him. One man was not enough to stop the legend. We were blessed indeed to have watched such a football maestro. He was a really great player, one of the best dribblers of his generation.

In the same team, Chapungu, there was also another gifted striker, fans called him the "Money Maker", his full

51

name was Wellington Shangiwa. This one was a tribute to his abilities to secure wins for his team, his goals ensured victory and his teammates would be smiling all the way to the bank. Every weekend was payday for them with "The Money Maker" in the team.

What about Archford Chimutanda, a mercurial and flawed genius. Chimutanda is regarded as one of the best midfielders to emerge from Zimbabwe. He had a locker full of football skills, ball control with virtually any part of his body, defence splitting passes and goals to add to the mix. He was a natural talent who made football such a joy to watch. However, Chimutanda lacked the commitment to train and his talent alone could not take him as far as he should have. But with his God given talents, he made fans happy, his passes were sweet, his goals dripped of honey and his ball control made them shout "Chehuche", the one as sweet as honey! It is a shame that one so good did not utilise his talent to its utmost level due to his off-the-field shenanigans. What a regret!

Other players are born to play football, they are born to score goals and Shackman Tauro was one such player, a goal machine. At the peak of his powers, he was a force of nature, a ruthless predator, in his pomp he was unplayable. Everyone knew that any ball in the box, Tauro attacked, any half chance Tauro buried, high ball, low ball, Tauro was at the end of it. He added variety to his goals and so opponents never knew how to handle him.

His predatory instincts made him one of the most feared strikers of his generation and I was fortunate enough to watch him train and play. Tauro was a finisher, pure and undiluted, goals were his DNA he was born to score! The fans came with a nickname "Mr. Goals!", how befitting. Another striker whose nickname matched his goal scoring exploits was Peter Nyama nicknamed "Thunderboots." He was a finisher with fierce shots, in the 1971 football season, he scored an incredible 62 goals, simply unbelievable! There was Maronga Nyangela, fans called him "The Bomber" and indeed he bombed the opposition goals with ruthless efficiency. Bomber in the opposition box was on a scorched earth mission, he took no prisoners, what a player!

"Tell them that TNT is back!" was the declaration that George Rollo, who played for Arcadia United in the late 70s, made after one match at Rufaro Stadium. What had happened? Well during that match Rollo had hit a ball so hard and hot that it tore the nets. The referee had to double check to satisfy himself that it was a goal. The gaping hole in the nets confirmed his fears, it was a goal that the bulging nets could not hold, it was too hot. This is the stuff of legends and indeed "TNT" was like dynamite, he exploded and those who were there would cherish the moment to this day – a true legend of the game. His goal scoring exploits resulted in him being crowned Soccer Star of 1978, ending the George Shaya winning streak of three consecutive titles.

The attitude of George Chirambarara earned him the nickname "Zero Zero". George had a never say die spirit and even when his team was losing which Fire Batteries Football Club usually did, he still believed that the team had a chance to turn the tables. Even when playing against the big guns, George believed that his team had an equal chance of winning, so the starting point was always a zero–zero score line.

It was a way of giving himself a fighting chance which is understandable because his team did not win many games. "We start on an equal footing and even when we are losing, it is not over until it is over!" is what he was saying. He needed to have that mental attitude when facing the big guns. Others whose nicknames depicted the mental attitude and strength were Mercedes "Rambo" Sibanda, Dumisani "Savimbi" Nyoni and Dumisani "Commando" Mpofu. These defenders never gave up, they were known for their fighting spirit and fans recognised this by coming up with these nicknames. Another defender with an interesting name was Frank Nyamukuta, nickname "The Dealer". As a young boy he went to stadiums to sell all sorts of food stuffs, "freezit, Maputi" and drinks. While others were busy enjoying the match , Frank would be making some money on the side. At school , he was always loaded with cash and his teacher simply called him "The Dealer". It stuck with him throughout his playing days!

Ebson Muguyo was considered as one of the best strikers to play in Zimbabwe, then known as Rhodesia and in South Africa. After he retired, he was inducted into the Kaiser Chiefs Hall of Fame, a confirmation of his football abilities. For this he was given the nickname "Sugar" indeed he was as sweet as sugar. He is not the only one who had this nickname, Mugove Munyorovi was also called "Sugar" His dribbling skills warranted this sweetsounding nickname although he was not as good as Ebson, the original" Sugar!"

Way before we knew about computers, fans gave Kenneth Jere the nickname "Computer" in 1984. Whoever gave him the nickname was ahead of his time, but it was a special nickname for a special talent. Jere was a dribbling wizard in the middle of the park, he was fast and threaded passes through the eye of a needle. He was a midfield maestro, a joy to watch for fans. Another with such perfect passes was Farai Mbidzo. He was a master of long-range pinpoint passes which always landed at the feet of a teammate. For this, the fans came up with a nickname "Mr. Perfect" because of his perfect passes.

Other nicknames are difficult to explain like "Rusty" for Eddison Lusengo, "Sinyo" for Stanley Ndunduma, "Sister" for Samson Choruwa. Others adopted the names of well-known politicians like former Masvingo United captain Godfrey Dondo who was burdened with the nickname "Mai Mahofa." I have tried to figure out, but I must confess the link is difficult to explain suffice to say that Mai Mhofa was renowned as the "Political Kingmaker" of Masvingo Province where she was a Governor. Maybe the nickname depicted the power that Godfrey also had in the Masvingo United Team.

Stanley Chirambadare was nicknamed "Samora" in reverence to the respected, but feared President of Mozambique Samora Machel. Chirambadare was a tough tackling defender, but his nickname was for his fight for the voice of the players to be heard. He fought for players' rights and led many strikes against the inept Dynamos administrators. To date, "Samora" still stands firm on his principles and his clarion call that football must be run well and that it should have a firm foundation. He is uncompromising in this regard and will not be silenced.

This fight for justice compounded by his keeping of a beard made comparisons with the legendary leader inevitable. "Kabila" the rebel cum leader of the Democratic Republic of Congo was given to Watson Muhoni and up and coming young defender whose death robbed Zimbabwe of a legend in the making. Steven Phiri was nicknamed "Biko" after the South African anti apartheid activist Steve Biko and "Savimbi" the Angola rebel leader was given to Dumisani Nyoni.

Other nicknames depicted the strength of the player, like Friday Phiri nicknamed" Breakdown", he had the strength of a breakdown truck which can pull other trucks. Misheck Marimo was known as" Scania," a tribute to all those tough trucks which used to ply our roads, they were known as Scanias. Ephraim Chawanda was known as the "Rock of Gibraltar," immovable in the heart of defence while Graham Boyle was known as the "Iron Man," solid and unbreakable. Sunday Marimo was known as "Never on Sunday" – an acknowledgement that no striker could get past him on a Sunday afternoon while Steve Chikodzi was known as "Cobra " for his painful cobra like tackles on the ankles.

James Matola was called "Van Damme "for his flying kicks and headers when defending. Others were given nicknames for doing well against certain football nations. Like George Mbwando nicknamed "Zambia" for doing well against Zambian Teams and Lazurus Muhoni nicknamed "Mali" for scoring against Mali, a football powerhouse in Africa. Incidents on international travels also led to some nicknames. Hardlife Zvirekwi lost all his luggage in Nairobi, Kenya and for that the name of the city became his second name, "Nairobi!" Joel Lupahla almost got on the wrong plane during an international trip, the plane was going to Dubai, fans did not let him forget this, he became known as "Dubai."

There was another nickname which took me a while to understand. Thulani Ncube was a very good defender for Highlanders, the Zimbabwe under 23 team and the Zimbabwe senior team. He was the type of modern defender that teams look for these days, one who is comfortable with both feet, can defend but can also pass the ball from the back.

Many defenders prefer to play it safe first but Thulani was brave enough to take the ball, look up and play a pass. He never panicked, Highlanders fans gave him the nickname "Biya". In my blissful ignorance, I just assumed that the moniker was borrowed from Republic of Cameroon long serving President General Paul Biya. I hope you can understand why, as earlier intimated we have often given our players the names of political leaders so Biya of Cameroon seemed a normal conclusion to make. A language lesson however awaited me! I am from the Shona ethnic group and my understanding of the Ndebele language is at best limited. With a better understanding of this language, I would have known that "biya" means fence in Ndebele or a protective wall usually for a field or a homestead. It was only after a discussion with a Ndebele friend that my mind opened to this hidden meaning. It was a revelation for me. Football had taught me a lesson. It is important to be familiar with the languages spoken in the country. Many of us do not do that and in the end, there are many misunderstandings. Thank you Thulani "Biya" for helping to open my eyes!

Another nickname which reflected the creativeness of our fans is that of Cephas Chimedza who was known as "Mai Chisamba!". Oh my God, our fans! How did that come about? Well in Zimbabwe, there is a popular Television Hostess renowned for her perceptive discussions on all social issues. She tackles topics as diverse as marital relationships, cultural topics and many other social challenges. There is no topic which is beyond Mai Chisamba and many Zimbabweans believe that if a topic is worth discussion, then it must be taken to Mai Chisamba's chat show and she will try to resolve it with her panellists.

How then does Cephas Chimedza fit into all this, how did he end up with the nickname "Mai Chisamba"? Well, Cephas was a good footballer. He was also versatile and could play at left back as well as an attacking midfielder. Fans came to rely on him and when the match became tough, he used to come up with the answers. Because of his ability to come up with match changing performances, fans decided to call him "Mai Chisamba." Indeed, like Mai Chisamba who solved many social topics, there was no football problem that Cephas could not solve. That dear reader explains the strange sounding nickname for the football maestro.

Other nicknames were drawn from musical hits. Oscar Motsi was a bundle of energy in the middle of the park for Caps United. He was the most enthusiastic player I have ever witnessed. When he burst onto the scene in 1985 the chart bursting song Simbimbino by the Bhundu

Boys was the song in Zimbabwe. Whether he loved the song very much, whether he played it always on the duke box during time out with friends, I am not sure, but Oscar Motsi became" Simbimbino". I always felt that the nickname fitted him like a glove because the song had a fast beat and Oscar played football at breakneck speed. He was so full of energy and truly enjoyed the game, he was bubbly and effervescent. Oscar played football with joy and to bring joy to the fans.

Another who found himself with a musical nickname was Blessing Makunike, he became known as "Yogo Yogo," a song by South African artist Penny Penny. It was a hit in Zimbabwe and again I can only speculate, maybe Makunike loved this song very much. What a player, he was a midfield maestro. The nickname had a nice ring to it," Yogo Yogo," it befitted a great player whose career was cut short in a tragic road accident.

Football and culture often mix and with that certain nicknames have been derived from totems and family clan names. Players who carried their whole clan name onto the field of play are Memory Mucherahova known as "Mwendamberi," while Sunday Marimo moved from "Never on Sunday" as a player to "Mhofu" when he became a coach, a popular totem in Zimbabwe. Bearers of the Mhofu clan pride themselves as having the success formula in life, Mhofus believe they can achieve anything. This theory seemed to be confirmed when Sunday Chizambwa became the first coach to lead Dynamos to a Champions league final in 1998 and Zimbabwe to an Afcon final tournament in Tunisia in 2004. It was a remarkable achievement giving weight to the much vaunted Mhofu clan success formula claim. Misheck Mapika was also known as "Shava" another prominent Shona totem.

I can not list them but some deserve special mention. Alexander Maseko of Highlanders was called "The Cool Ruler " and Ernest Mutano of Dynamos and Black Rhinos was known as "Mr. Cool" Both monikers were a tribute to their calm disposition when in possession of the ball, they never panicked. Three other legends carried nicknames which resoanated with the packed stadiums. Willard Khumalo, nicknamed " Mahwii", Dumisani Mpofu known as " Commando" and Henry Charles , "Beefy" were popular with the fans. Every time they had the ball, the fans would respond by chanting their nicknames. "Mahwiiiiiii!", "Commandoooooo!" or " Beefeeee!" were common sounds which emanated from the crowd. It was all part of our football culture further revealing how these were our heroes.

While most nicknames are positive, some of them can be cruel. Max Lunga was a capable striker who scored many goals, but his lack of pace was often used as a stick to beat him with. Fans being fans came up with the nickname" Sikorokoro" a far from pleasing one to the legend. Dear reader, a Sikorokoro is an old car which is on its last wheels. Obviously, speed cannot be a feature of this car so Lunga's anger is more than understandable.

Simon Dambaza was regarded as a super sub who rescued many matches for my favourite team Caps United. He was heavily built, he looked more like a wrestler than a football player. For this, fans gave him the nickname Yokozuna after the Japanese sumo wrestlers. I am sure the legend was far from happy with this. And imagine giving a player the nickname "Satan", that was Prince Mbara who played for Kambuzuma United, Dynamos and Shooting Stars for you. I bet he hated it!

However, it will be an anomaly if I wrap up this football experience without talking about one of the most interesting characters to grace our league, Never Chiku. He was a man who could change a game in a blink of an eye especially when he came on as a substitute. His predatory instincts earned him the nickname

"Maswerasei." This might leave some of us a puzzled as to where that came from.

Well it is an interesting story befitting his colourful football career. For indeed, he had a colourful football life. Here is a man who was once called to the National team after his rich vein of form had drawn the attention of the coaches. He deserved it! However, when the time came to travel, there was a bombshell, our good legend did not have passport. Not only did he not have a passport, he did not have a birth certificate, he did not have a national identity card. In the records of the country, Never Chiku did not exist. "Who is Never Chiku?" was the bold Headline in the papers. Some papers simply called him "The Ghost!" The Register General had to run around to try and help Never, it is an incident embedded in our football narrative.

Anyway, back to how the nickname came about. When Never was terrorising defenders in the late 80's, there was also a lion in the Kariba region which was also terrorising villagers, animals and proving to be elusive to capture for the game rangers. It was indeed a terror to all. The headline talked about Maswersei, the lion of Kariba! Our creative fans still managed to come up with a nickname amidst the terror so Never Chiku became "Maswerasei." The fear that he struck in defenders was the same as that of the old lion of Kariba, Maswerasei!

Nicknames are indeed a part and parcel of our football folklore. I have left out a lot of them and have just presented the most interesting one. I hope the fans will continue putting on their creative hats on and churn them out, from "Daidzaivamwe" to" Nsukusonke," nicknames make the football story so much fun. Often, they are the story within the story.

I say Long may it continue!

Chapter 6
Dribbling Wizards

Dribbling is an art which seems to have been sacrificed on the altar of tactical discipline. Coaches these days are literally suspicious of players who indulge themselves and try to entertain the fans. Winning is more important than entertaining. We live in an age of possession football and giving away the ball has become a cardinal sin. To dribble, players need to be courageous and there are a few who still dare to dribble. Players like Lionel Messi, Ronaldo, Neymar on the international stage still try the audacious skills, but I think it is safe to say gone are the days of Sir Stanley Mathews who was known as the wizard of the wing.

Gone too are the days of Zidane who played football as if he was "playing with his hands" according to one of his admirer, David Beckham. Yes, we were blessed to watch Ronaldinho performing the " elastico dribble" and our very own African legend Jay Jay Okocha toying with opponents at will with the ball at his feet.

"When I went to Europe I said to myself, I will dribble them until they chop grass!" Okocha once said in an interview. The list of master dribblers on the international stage is long. In Zimbabwe, we were spoiled too, there were so many great dribblers and it is to them that I dedicate this chapter.

Just a cursory look at the pre-independence era, we have had so many dribbling wizards. I did not watch them, but I have heard mouth watering tales about these stars from football elder historians who never miss an opportunity to talk about these slippery greats. It will be amiss not to comment briefly about these legends.

Like Patrick Dzvene nicknamed "Amato the Devil" for his daring and endless tricks on the wing. He was a Dynamos founding member but stayed with the club for only six months. Those of an older generation still attest that his dribbling prowess was as good as that of Brazilian dribbling legend Garricha. Now this is some comparison! Before football became big business, players played for fun and to entertain fans. Patrick was a bundle of tricks and it is not hyperbole to compare him with the Brazilian legend. His skills earned him a move to Ndola United of Zambia.

He became the first black player to play outside the country way back in the 1960's. At Ndola United, he played so well that Aston Villa the England giants came knocking intending to sign the dribbling master. This a clear testament of the impact that he had made. However, because of the sporting sanctions which were imposed on Rhodesia because of her racist policies, the deal fell through. What a shame for indeed the skills of this legend deserved to grace a higher stage.

I have already talked about George Shaya nicknamed "The Mastermind" a man who often took football matters into his own hands by changing the game in an instant. Shaya had a magical right foot and tales are told about how defenders would literally fall sick on the eve of a match to avoid facing the wizard. Shaya was a terror to many defenders due to his endless bag of tricks.

During the seventies, football was brutal, the pitches were not the best and defenders often took the man with the ball. "If you miss the ball do not miss the man!" was the simple message which was often imparted to the defenders. To take on defenders therefore was to put one's body on the firing line literally. It needed courage, the courage to be audacious. Shaya often reduced these tough tackling defenders to mere spectators as he glided past them.

He was a slippery as an eel and fans often left the stadium shaking their heads in awe of the magic that they would have witnessed. With the ball at his feet, The Mastermind was simply a gift from heaven. Among his peers, the likes of Majuta "Jujuju" Mpofu, bulky but with skills galore, the diminutive Bernard Zikhali, ten times Soccer Star of the year finalist Joseph Zulu, David George the man who was known as "Broom boy" and David Madondo to mention a few were also dribbling royalty.

Mukoma Laban Kandi, the former Dynamos, Zimbabwe Saints and Rio Tinto goalkeeper told me a story about Robert Godoka, the man he claims introduced the step over into Zimbabwe (Rhodesia) football way back in the seventies.

"Robert Godoka was ahead of his time, he did the step over skill before we knew about the existence of the skill!" said Mukoma Laban. Apparently, when he first did at in a match at Gwanzura Stadium, everyone was taken by surprise and started imitating it. "The skill spread like wild fire in the league but went further than that." said Mukoma Laban. "At weddings there was a dance which became known as the Godoka, it was an attempt to incorporate the step over into the wedding dance routines, KuGodoka we called it." Mukoma Laban added leaving me bemused. What an impact that the legend had.

In 1981, as earlier stated my journey into football fandom began and yes, I watched some great dribblers at various stadiums. One of my favourite players from Dynamos even without being a Dynamos fan was Edward Katsvere nicknamed "Madhobha or Twinkle toes." He had a special skill and it was a unique one, I have since named it "The Madhobha Dribble" and it often left defenders for dead. As a winger, Katsvere had the licence to dribble and indeed he dribbled with aplomb. He was able to hold on to the ball, pretend to be pushing it forward and then drag it back again to himself. Words cannot adequately describe this skill but when he did that drag back, he left defenders tackling thin air. With the defender on his backside, Madhobha would streak down the line to send in an inviting cross for his strikers to bury home. What a skill that was, one manufactured and perfected in the motherland, the "Madhobha dribble"! The legendary defender, Graham Boyle among others always struggled against this skill and often enough he never finished the game without a caution. Katsvere gave him a torrid time, how he hated to play against this fair skinned diminutive football legend.

I have already talked about Maxmillion Ndlovu simply known as Boy for his boyish good looks so I will give him a pass and let me talk about Mike Abrahams the one we called "Mabhurugwa" because he used to wear very big shorts. He played his football on the touchline and it was here where he did most of damage. He kept the ball glued to his feet as he streaked down the touchline leaving defenders in his wake and for that he earned the title the "Touchline Magician" Defenders feared him and so did opposition fans.

I remember on one occasion Dynamos fans nicodemously went to his house in Mufakose to threaten him before one cup final. It was visitation inspired by a fear, the fear of embarrassment that he was likely to cause their team the next day. On this occasion, the intimidation tactics worked, he had a poor game, maybe that was the only way to stop the magician. On any other day, he used to tear defenders to shreds with his amazing skills. He was a bag full of tricks and defenders did not know how to handle him.

Players like Stanford Mtizwa nicknamed "Stix" for his slim built during youthful days, he has since gained weight, also had some amazing dribbling skills. I must mention something special about this midfield maestro. His ball control was impeccable especially with his chest. Apart from this skill, Mtizwa was also a master of the dribble especially from midfield. Having controlled the ball with his chest, Mtizwa used his bagful of skills to leave defenders baffled before releasing those defence splitting passes which were also his trademark. Kenneth Jere was another great dribbler and the nickname "Computer" captured this. Jere was a fast thinker and an expert manipulator of the ball. He loved to dribble from midfield and he often eliminated opponents with a drop of the shoulder, a swivel of the waist before passing the ball into space. He never ran out of ideas, what a midfielder he was.

Vitalis Takawira nicknamed "Digital" was another notable dribbler. One match will live long in the memory of most Zimbabweans, the four to one mauling of the Indomitable Lions of Cameroon. Vitalis helped himself to a hatrick but it was the way he went about it which will be etched in the football memories of many. He literally rang rings around the Lions defence, tormenting the defenders at will with his repertoire of skills. One Cameroon defender could not take it anymore and had to leave the pitch in tears having been given a red card for persistent fouling. On many occasions in the league Vitalis always put in some stellar performances and local defenders lived in constant fear of the menace paused by this slippery winger. To rub salt into the wounds of opposing teams, he scored goals by the hatful. The nickname "Digital" was a tribute to his mesmerising skills. I think in the Zimbabwe football fraternity, Vitalis is among the top five dribblers of all time. On his day, he was simply unplayable.

Morgan Nkatazo or "Mogiza" as the fans called him was another who was blessed with silky dribbling skills. In 1996 when Caps United were pushing for their first League title after independence, Morgan was a thorn in the flesh of many defenders. The team was blessed with a galaxy of attacking talents, Alois Bunjira, Stewart Murisa, Felix Antonio and super sub Simon "Yokozuna" Dambaza.

While the above four were out and out strikers whose focus was to score goals, Morgan was the tormentor in chief, he decorated the attacking play with mazy dribbling runs. In the end Caps United clinched the league, fans will always remember this team but above all they will cherish the devastating and entertaining dribbling skills of Morgan "Mogiza" Nkhatazo.

Many fans in the Zimbabwe football fraternity will swear by the name of Moses Chunga who played for Dynamos, the man known as the" Razorman." He arrived from Lyton Wolves as a virtual unknown but before long everyone was singing his name. He announced himself at Dynamos in 1983, with a bang and kept fans on the edge of their seats and defenders on their toes. His many faithful followers declare that he added at least a million supporters to the seven million claimed Dynamos supporters. Many fans simply came to watch Moze or "Razorman" as they called him play. Opposition fans hated him, defenders were in awe of him.

When in full flow, it was difficult for anyone to get the ball from his feet. He had a habit of confusing defenders with endless leg over tricks, it was simply unbelievable what he was able to do with the ball at his feet. We were blessed to watch Moses play. Before FIFA the world football body decided to ban players from standing on top of the ball, Chunga used to do that bringing the whole stadium to its feet. What a talent he was!

Another player who announced himself with a bang as a fresh faced young man was Peter Ndlovu who played for Highlanders Football Club. Mukoma Francis Nechironga, the former Caps United, Rio Dairiboard and Arcadia bustling striker told me a story about Peter. Sunday Marimo the then Dynamos gaffer said to his defenders "Henry Charles, Angirai Chapo", listen, we are going to Bulawayo, there is a young man at Highlanders, he is a dribbling wizard, make sure you keep him away as far away as possible from the box," he stressed.

When the match started, the defenders could do little to stop Peter. The then 18 year old tormented the veteran defenders and during the return match, the coach was forced change his defence line up. Peter could conjure a moment of magic and often this led to a goal. Like the goal he scored against South Africa at the National Sports Stadium, a moment of magic which will go down in Zimbabwe football history as one as the best scored at the giant National Sports Stadium. Be patient dear reader for I will describe this goal in greater detail later in this narrative. It deserves special attention! When he moved to England to play for Coventry in 1991, The English press called him the "Bulawayo Bullet" or "The Flying Elephant" – both monikers a tribute to his amazing skills. Peter used to dribble, and he dribbled at pace. Very few defenders could stop him.

Stanley Manyati who played for Dynamos and Dairiboard Football Club, was, called him "Chola" after the great Zambian footballer Alex Chola was also a master dribbler. Chola had a magical right foot, he specialised in what we called in our local parlance the "mbama" or a drag of the ball in a semi-circular way which often left defenders on their backside. Chola deployed this skill regularly and the packed ground would respond with chants of "Cholaaaaaaa!"

It was also a skill used by Shadreck "Waga Waga "Dzvairo especially at his favourite hunting ground, Gwanzura Stadium. The crowd would respond with the "Wagaaaaaaaaaaaaaaaaaa." chant. What sweet memories indeed! Shadreck was from Highfield, I knew him well and it is always good to see someone you know performing some football magic. In Highfield, "Waga Waga" was a cult hero because he played for Black Aces. Later Black Aces had another dribbling hero, Nqobizitha Ncube; fans gave him the nickname" Pengaudzoke" because of his impeccable body swerves. His coach Mac Duvillard instructed him to dribble and this he did with devastating effect.

There was Johanes Ngodzo of Highlanders whose dribbling wizardry earned him the nickname" Signature." Cruel injury cut short his career and I keep wondering how far he could have gone! Injury also cut short the career of Basil Chisopo of Caps United. He was another tricky customer and fans ended up calling him "Chisipo "a play on his name to suggest that he was as slippery as a soap. Indeed, defenders found him hard to handle.

I remember the likes of Lewis Kutinyu, Austin "Masebho" Juwayeyi, Machona "Gweje Gweje" Sibanda, Joseph Machingura, Joseph Kabwe, Usman "Uchi" Misi, Mandla Balanda, and Allan Jalasi, Tutani "Toots" Moyo, Mugove Munyorovi among others who were a terror to defenders. Joseph Kabwe in particular was a great dribbler; many tales are told of how he swept past defenders as if they did not exist. Unfortunately, for fans, he did not stay long to reach his full potential preferring instead to pursue further studies in the United States of America. I just wonder how far he could have gone with his football if he had stayed on for a few more years. Thomas Muchanyarei and Garikayi Zuze also deserve to sit on this high table of renowned dribblers in the Zimbabwe football fraternity. They deserve to dine with the best.

Yes, dribbling is an art, which is like second nature to many Zimbabwe players. Some seem to be born with it and they simply have a natural flair. Players like Nkulumo Donga, Mugove Munyorovi, Tauya Murehwa, Thomas Muchanyarei, David Malunga, Collins Kabote, Samson Choruwa and Takaitei Muswe were all dribbling masters. Some relied on the body swerve, others on ball manipulation and yet others deployed a variety of skills, often leaving defenders on the deck. They made football such a joy to watch. Let me talk briefly about one man on that list of dribbling wizards, Tauya Murehwa.

The body swerve can be devastating if used effectively and one man who used this with aplomb was Tauya "Doctor" Murehwa. He was nicknamed Doctor because when burst into the limelight he was studying to be a doctor at the University of Zimbabwe. On the pitch, Tauya was a football doctor. He often picked up the ball and embarked on mazy runs leaving defenders on their backside with cheeky body swerves. They were a joy to watch even for rival fans. To face Tauya in full flow was to be taken to the cleaners. Defenders knew it and they had to use unorthodox means to try to stop him.

From the dusty streets in the townships to the primary and secondary schools up to the then Super league and later the Zimbabwe Premier Soccer league, our football is stocked with dribbling stars who entertained us with their God given talents. It is such shame that the art of dribbling is slowly being discouraged by many coaches who have now adopted the win at all cost approach. Players are also afraid to improvise, they play to the coach's instructions and in the end, they deliver robotic performances. The audacious skills of past football greats are slowly being consigned to the memories of those fans who were old enough to witness them. It is such a shame because indeed, there will always be a special place in the hearts of fans for players who excel in the art of dribbling!

Chapter 7
Football songs and football skills

"When you walk through a storm, hold your head high, and do not be afraid of the dark... Walk on through the wind. Walk on through the rain... Walk on with hope in your heart... And you will never walk Alone...!"

No song is as closely linked to a football club as "You will never walk alone", a song turned into a Liverpool Club anthem by Gary and the Pacemakers. Although Gary did not write the original song, he can be credited with introducing it to the Liverpool Football Club hierarchy who were so impressed that they adopted it as their motivational song. It is a song of triumph over adversity. The song has also been adopted by Celtic Football Club and Borrusia Dortmund. However, for the emotional pull of this song, one need not look any further than Anfield Road, the home of Liverpool Football club.

Yes, music and football mix well all over the world and that song "You will never walk alone" is one of those emotional ones which connects the players on the pitch and the fans in the terraces. Where there is football there is music, from the primary school kids standing by the touchline singing songs of praise for their heroes on the dusty pitches to grown up men and women gyrating to the rhythms of music at most stadiums. I love music, all genres with Chimurenga, reggae and sungura topping my list. I can write a whole chapter on my favourite musicians both at home and abroad. For the purposes of this chapter, let me just focus on the football related songs.

When we were growing up we sang songs to encourage ourselves as we embarked on our football trips. One song that I remember very well reflected our total commitment to football, our preparedness even to die for the game. We sang "Amai nababa, musandicheme, kana ndafa, ne bhora! Ndini ndakazvida, kutamba bhora pamwe chete nevamwe… My parents do not mourn for me if I die while playing football, it is my choice!" an unequivocal and clarion declaration of our commitment to the game of football. We had made a choice to play and our commitment was total.

There are many such songs that are sang and most of them have become part of our football folklore. From "Dynamos baba, haina ngozi" to "Kepekepe bhora" these songs are used to motivate the players and to keep the morale high among the supporters. Fans in the stands compose songs to encourage their teams and the songs often embody the creative nature of the fans. Most of these songs remain unrecorded but they are passed on from one generation of fans to another. "Kepe Kepe Bhora!" for example has become a club anthem for Caps United Football club and every generation of supporters is familiar with this one.

On the other hand, there are other songs that have been recorded to laud the exploits of football clubs and their players in the world and Zimbabwe is not an exception. Several artists have tried their hand, some with great success, others not so. Some of the songs are very emotional and because they are rather old, they create a lot of nostalgia as they capture the glory years of the team. These songs transport the listeners to those years when big stars used to mesmerise fans in our leagues.

Many artists have contributed to this genre in Zimbabwe. In my humble opinion, I think Mukoma Zexie Manatsa has done more to raise the bar in this regard. The man is one of the veterans of the Zimbabwe music scene who has penned such chart busters like "Chipo Chiroorwa" and the controversial "Tea Hobvu," among others and like most people in this beautiful but troubled nation, he loves his football. He has shown this by

71

producing a number of songs, most of them classics. These include "Makepeke Shaisa Mufaro, Highlanders Iwinile, Tamirira Dynamos Igowese and Zimbabwe Saints." These songs were hits when they were first produced and up to now they still appeal to the ear and the emotions. Listening to them brings the memories flooding back, they connect many fans with a glorious past of our football.

Zimbabwe Saints were a great football institution. They were a part of the football culture before and after independence. This great club now wallows in the unfashionable world of lower league football and are threatened with extinction. It has been a painful fall from grace, a fall brought about by poor leadership and power-hungry individuals.This pains me a lot but let me not digress, the power struggles deserve a separate chapter, time permitting. In 1988, Zimbabwe Saints played some of the best football ever seen in the Zimbabwe league. They went for twenty-three matches unbeaten on their way to the league championship. They were unstoppable. This amazing season gave rise to Mukoma Zexie's song "Zimbabwe Saints" in which he lauds their playing style, their pass and move one touch football.

Mukoma Zexie says, "Vakomana vanotamba bhora sevanotamba tsoro...ukadyiwa ne Saints wadyiwa ne bhobho." Literally translated it means "These lads play football as if they are playing checkers" The analogy is interesting, he could not have captured it any better. The coaches Tendai Chieza and Roy Barretto insisted on the ball staying on the floor, players passed it around until they scored. It was tiki taka before Barcelona introduced us to this term. Saints were ahead of their time and credit should go to the above-mentioned coaches. Credit should also go to the players who were brave enough to play this type of football. Players like big goalkeeper John Sibanda and Pernell Mackop, playing from the back, defenders like

Ephraim Chawanda, Misheck Sibanda, and Josphat Humbasha.

What about midfielders like Chemi Hunidzarira, Norman Gumbo, Obey Sova, George Ayibu , captain Jimmy Phiri and attackers like Henry Mackop, Joseph Machingura, Mayor Eric among others. This was football at its most breathtaking and Mukoma Zexie was also captivated and converted. He became a disciple like most of us and that song expressed his gratitude to the team. Now the team is unrecognisable from these glory years, it is a shell of its former self. Cry the beloved Saints, I hope they bounce back, they need new leaders to achieve that! Bring back Chikwata that is my football prayer every time I think of those hey days of Chauya Chikwata Zimbabwe Saints.

Mukoma Zexie also sang another classic, "Makepeke Shaisa Mufaro" for Caps United and what a song it is. It is a must-listen for any football loving Zimbabwean and even beyond. Just like fans have fallen in love with "You Will Never Walk Alone" worldwide, I think this song can also resonate with fans on the world stage. They may not understand the words, but they cannot ignore the rhythm. This song captures the Caps United heydays when they were known as the "Cup kings."

With Dynamos dominating the league, Caps United decided to focus on the cup games. They could lose an easy match in the league but come the next weekend, they would be on fire if it was a cup game. Francis Nechironga, the bustling Caps United player of the early 80's let me onto the secret. Apparently, the officials at Caps United agreed with the players that they could share the winnings of any cup competition. For this reason, the players were motivated as compared to the league games when they were given a fixed amount.

The club became cup game specialists, the Zifa Castle Cup, they won it so many times that they were asked to keep the trophy. The Rothmans Cup, Chibuku Trophy, Rosebowl cup, they collected them all. The song captures this very well and what a song. I love it and I will never tire of listening to it. "Makepekepe, shaisa Mufaro, Makepe huya uzovaona...", a translation will not do justice to this song, it is there to be listened to!

The music legend did not end there, he also penned and sang another classic "Tamirira Dynamos Igowese..." this song does one thing for me, it reminds me of the great players who have come and gone. I will always remember and cherish them. It is a great song, an important historical document.

Mukoma Zexie Manatsa saved his best for last. "Highlanders Iwinile.." What a song! I love this song and even a diehard rival supporter cannot help but dance to this song. This is a song which can make grown up men and women cry, it has that impact! It is a song which can win a club new converts. Rival supporters can dance to this song and it is the type of song which brings supporters together.

Following hard on the legend's heels is Mukoma Lovemore Majaivana whose song "Badlala njani" sends some shivers down my back. I really feel this song, it captures the heart and soul of the club. It is a song which brings Highlanders Football Club to the heart of the listener. It is a song which will transport one to Babourfields, Makokoba, Pumula, Nkulumane, to every suburb in the City of Kings. It is a song which brings back good memories and also sad emotions about the great players we have lost.

Titus Majola, Nhamo Shambira, Tymon Mabaleka and Willard Khumalo. During their heydays, they gave us joy! I once suggested that this song must be made the club anthem of Highlanders Football club. I think anyone who listens to this song will appreciate what the club is all about. It is a more than a club, it is the people and the people are the club. The two are inseparable, they are like fish and water. I am sure if anything ever happens to Highlanders Football Club, some people will just die, death by suicide and this is no hyperbole.

I have friends who live and breathe Highlanders Football club. They tell me often, without the team their lives are meaningless. They tell me that when faced with a depressing situation, they turn to the song to uplift their spirits. It is a song which reminds them of what this club means, it is more than a club! Mukoma Lovemore Majaivana also dedicated one song to slain midfield powerhouse Titus Majola. His death struck all fans across the football divide with grief and that song united everyone in their grief.

The Real Sounds of Africa also penned an interesting song. "Dynamos versus Tornadoes." This song has a rhumba beat because the group had settled in Zimbabwe from the Democratic Republic of Congo. It is a good song, more so because of the commentary of Charles Mabika which is embedded in it. I think it is an original commentary or if it is an imitation, then it is a very good one. Anyway, the point is that this song makes the reader live the match and enjoy, it is vividly narrated. Chimurenga music guru, Thomas "Muchadura" Mapfumo whose hard hitting, political lyrics have forced him into exile decided to make his football contribution with the song "Shumba Dzenhabvu". This was a song dedicated to the 1998 World Cup in France. Once more Charles Mabika, lends his voice to the commentary, that is the icing on the cake. Very enjoyable indeed! I can also add Tanga Wekwa Sando who sang a dedication to the "Zimbabwe National Team" Vakomana Vekwedu". The song captures the hey days of the Dream team under Fabisch, the period when we packed the National Sports Stadium to cheer them on. These were happy days and cherished memories.

Music and football are a powerful a deadly combination indeed. Football is the national game in Zimbabwe, just as it is in most countries in Africa and the world over. Music is the soul of life and when music and football come together, the experience can be unforgettable. Dear reader, if you doubt this, listen to "Badlala njani" by Lovemore Majaivana, if that does not persuade you, then nothing will. Even a heart of stone will melt after listening to this song, a tear or two will not be out of place here.

Now that I have talked about this special ingredient of music which captures the heart and soul of Zimbabwe football, allow me to sample the special skills which our football stars made their trademark. Consider this dear reader, on the international stage, we have the panenka, the Zidane shuffle and the Ronaldinho elastico, these are special skills made famous by these great players. Well our players did not invent football but there are certain skills that they mastered so well that the skill became synonymous with them.

When we were growing up, we often talked about the chest control as "the Mtizwa control ". We were enthralled by the way he used to "silence" the ball with his chest. We said "silenced" because the ball did not move an inch once he had it under control. His magical touch allowed him to keep the ball glued on his chest until he decided to drop it down to his feet for further special treatment before he released one of his killer passes. Stanford Mtizwa was a football genius who could control the ball with any part of his body, it was with his chest that he was an expert. For this reason, we always tried to perfect the chest control, in our minds it was the ultimate ball control skill which had to be mastered. Mastering it usually secured a place in the team, it was a rite of passage for most of the young boys. Whenever I think of the chest control, I think of this evergreen football maestro Stanford "Stix" Mtizwa.

Another skill, which fascinated us as youngsters, was the throughball often given with the outside of the foot. We called it the "Outfooter pass" but I admit that I have not seen the word used anywhere else. In official football manuals it is known as "the outside of the foot pass" or "the side foot pass". Our fascination with this pass stemmed from watching the mercurial football maestro Archford Chimutanda. I have already talked about Chimutanda who was considered by many as a flawed genius because of his prodigious talent but also for his poor attitude to training. What defined Archie however was his ability to split defences with one through pass.

Often enough he delivered the perfect through ball which made it so easy for the striker to score. His passes were a gift to the striker and that is why he often boasted "Tinokupai makeke emapass motadza zvenyu...i give you gift wrapped passes but you fail to score..." Yes, Archie was as good with his feet as he was with his sarcastic tongue. He did not hesitate to mock his teammates if he felt that they were not up to his expected standard. Since he was so good, he expected everyone to be at the same wavelength with him. He did not hesitate to proclaim "Ndiri kutamba ndega. I am playing alone, implying that none of them were up to his standard."

This was a damning assessment of his colleagues. As young boys, we could not get enough of Archie or Mukoma Archie as we used to call him, his passes made him a cult hero in our eyes. Flawed genius yes but allow me reader to name the through ball in the Zimbabwe football fraternity, "the Chimutanda pass" or to borrow from his sweet-sounding nickname, the "Chehuchi pass" for indeed his passes were as sweet as honey. He was able to see a pass where others could not, he created space where there was no space. Think of a pass as a gift as

77

another mercurial genius Eric Cantona said years later, then in the Zimbabwe football fraternity, think Archie Chimutanda. What a player!

When it came to ball juggling there was one man for the job, Joel Shambo and as kids we tried to do "a Shambo" at any given opportunity. "The Headmaster" as we knew him was a master ball juggler and whenever he got the ball he never missed the opportunity to entertain the crowd. His juggling was purposeful, and he used it to advance into space before creating a chance for his teammates. Watching Shambo in full flow enhanced our football skills and aspirations. We used to challenge each other and the one who perfected would captain the team for the day.

For this reason, give me the leeway to name the ball juggling skills in our football fratenity the "Shambo Control" In the same breath let me also talk about a player whose ball control was amazing but also specialised in one effective skill, the dummy. Lloyd Mutasa or "Samaita" as we knew him was indeed a master of the dummy which often left opponents going one way and he going another. He used it again and again and each time he did the crowd would rise to salute a master of deception. The dummy when executed to perfection can best be described as poetry in motion. It represents football intelligence, it is the triumph of the brain over brawn.

On many occasions, Lloyd Mutasa would let the ball roll between his legs allowing him to pass to a teammate without touching the ball. The way he executed these moves showed his football intelligence and for that, I will not hesitate to call the dummy the "Samaita" move. Samaita as earlier stated was his nickname. I am sure many who have followed Zimbabwe football will agree with me.

There are many skills which footballers mastered from an early age. In the Zimbabwe football fraternity one such skill was "the mbama", I have found no English equivalent to the name. I will try to describe it as much as I can. This skill is usually used by wingers who can drag the ball in a half circle away from the defender. This fast movement of the ball often leaves the defender on his backside allowing the winger the space and time to deliver a good cross. Several players in the Zimbabwe football fraternity used this skill but from my memory, the master of this was Stanley "Chola" Manyati. He used this skill so effectively that it will not be amiss for me to call it the "Manyati dribble."

The nutmeg is used universally but the man who perfected it in Zimbabwe was Boy Ndlovu the dribbling wizard. He used it with devastating effect and many defenders if they had a choice would put small nets between their legs to stop the ball from going through. Comic yes, but that was the only way to stop Boy from humiliating them. For this reason, let me give Boy Ndlovu this one. I have also talked about the "Madhobha Dribble" in the previous chapter, the one perfected by Edward Katvere and for that let me name this one after him.

Indeed, many skills have been used by our players and even as youngsters, we tried to emulate them. Mastering these routines became part and parcel of our football DNA. It is the way we learnt our football, the way we enjoyed our football, and the way we understood our football. Yes, football is a universal sport, a universal language but trust me dear reader we had our own unique way of celebrating it and talking about it. From skills such as the "Mbama" and the "Madhobha dribble" to the music, we indeed have a unique Zimbabwe way. This chapter is a tribute to both!

Dribling Wizard Johannes "Signature" Ngodzo on the ball

Edward Katsvere, nicknamed Madhobha, dribbling wizard

The best match I watched in 1987... Caps United vs Black Rhinos

The man who made me a football disciple, Joel Shambo with former President of Zimbabwe, Rev. Canaan Banana

Midfield genius ... Archford "Chehuche" Chimutanda

Soccer Star of the year Calendar... This was 1980

My wife Tendai... Since 1992

My young brother Clement, he was a good defender

Legendary Dynamos Football Club supporters... Freddy Pasuwa Mugadza with bandage

Jean Betrand Bocande of Senegal, he destroyed Zimbabwe in 1985

National Team 1992... they caused a National Heartbreak

A stubborn supporter making his voice heard

Football great Peter Ndlovu represented Zimbabwe well in England

Football fans in Zimbabwe

Caps United in 1981

Football fans go through a lot of emotional pain

My wife Tendai

Evans Mambara, a great football commentator

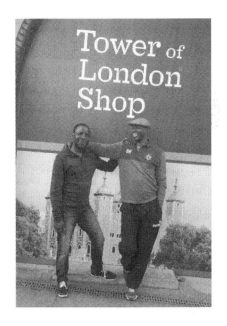

My brother Richard and I

National Team

My sister Ngaakudzwe

Trip to Australia.. Happy memories!

Family... with son Tinashe

History makers... The Zimbabwe National Team which
qualified for Afcon 2004

Youthful days...

THE crack "Bosso" side of the 80s . . . Standing (from left): Sydney Zimunya, Titus Majola (late), Simon Ncube, Douglas Mloyi, Cephas Sibanda, Alexander Maseko, Netsai Moyo, Nqobizitha Maenzanise, Tanny Banda, Willard Kumalo, Peter Nkomo. Crouching (from left): Tobias Mudyambanje, Dumisani Nyoni, Mercedes Sibanda, Madinda Ndlovu, Fanuel Ncube (late), Abraham Madondo, Thoko Sithole

Strong Team... Highlanders F.C.

A strong Dynamos Football Club...

94

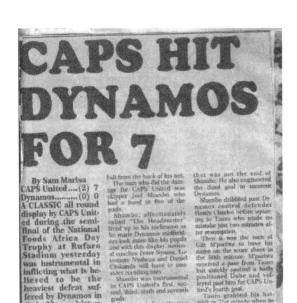

CAPS HIT DYNAMOS FOR 7

By Sam Marisa

CAPS United .... (2) 7
Dynamos .... (0) 0

A CLASSIC all round display by CAPS United during the semi-final of the National Foods Africa Day Trophy at Rufaro Stadium yesterday was instrumental in inflicting what is believed to be the heaviest defeat suffered by Dynamos in

ball from the back of his net. The man who did the damage for CAPS United was skipper Joel Shambo who had a hand in five of the goals.

Shambo, affectionately called "The Headmaster" lived up to his nickname as he made Dynamos midfielders look more like his pupils and with this display, national coaches Peter Nyama, Lovemore Nyabeza and Daniel Chikanda will have to consider recalling him.

Shambo was instrumental in CAPS United's first, second, third, sixth and seventh goals.

that was not the end of Shambo. He also engineered the third goal to torment Dynamos.

Shambo dribbled past Dynamos central defender Henry Charles before squaring to Tauro who made no mistake just two minutes after resumption.

Then it was the turn of Gift Mparwa to have his name on the score sheet in the 50th minute. Mparwa received a pass from Tauro but quickly spotted a badly positioned Dube and volleyed past him for CAPS United's fourth goal.

Tauro grabbed his hat-trick in 71st minute when he

Big Result for Caps United

Grassroots Pitches have been neglected

95

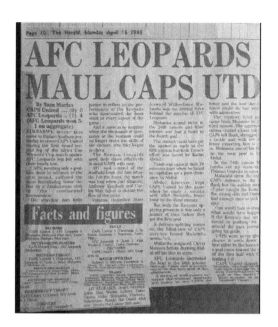

Bad Day in the office...

Dream Team... It raised our hopes but failed to qualify

Shacky Tauro was called Mr. Goals

Nkulumo Donga, right, was called Daidzaivamwe

Chapter 8
The international arena: The highs and lows!

On 16 August 1992, I watched one of the best
international matches ever played at the National Sports
Stadium. I also watched one of the best goals ever scored
by a Zimbabwean National Team player. It marked the
beginning of a dream, a dream which almost became a
reality before Kalusha Bwalya brought us thudding back to
earth a year later, on the 25th of July 1993, with that cruel
equalising header.

Cruel in our eyes for we had invested emotionally in
this Dream Team we even forgot that maybe the Zambian
Stars who perished in that Gabon plane crush were smiling
from heaven because their deaths were not in vain.
Kalusha did it for his departed comrades but for the
multitude of Zimbabweans who thronged the National
Sports Stadium, it was a fatal blow. Mixed emotions yes
but let me talk about this beautiful goal first.

When South Africa were finally readmitted into the
International Sporting community in 1992 after years of
isolation for the country's racist policies, Bafana Bafana as
the National team was known, rolled into town to face
our very own recently christened "Dream Team."
Zimbabwe had just appointed a fiery German coach,
Reinhard Fabisch with Roy Barreto and Sunday Marimo as
his assistants. A group of players at their peak led by
Ephraim Chawanda were brought together to start the
dream journey. These were great players, Mercedes
Sibanda, Melusi Nkiwane, Francis Shonhayi, Memory
Mucherahowa, Adam Ndlovu, a young Peter Ndlovu,
Vitalis Takawaira, Rahman Gumbo, Agent Sawu and indeed

the Jungleman Bruce Grobelaar who ended years of self imposed exile to join the journey.

There are many who joined in later, but these were the pioneers. To spice it up, there was controversy, the exclusion of crowd favourite Moses "Razorman" Chunga whom the coach felt was an unnecessary luxury. Many fans especially those who supported Dynamos were unhappy with this ruthless football decision. They felt that Fabisch was anti Dynamos. My best friend Francis Garaba was one of those who joined in this anti Fabisch brigade. Some neutral fans were also unhappy but Fabisch stuck to his guns. To date the debate still rages on, should he have included Moze? Opinion is still divided close to thirty years later!

South African and Zimbabwean football are closely interlinked and even during those years of isolation, Zimbabwe fans knew a lot of South African players. They also knew a lot about South African teams such as Kaiser Chiefs, Mamelodi Sundowns and yes one of the most supported foreign clubs in Zimbabwe, Orlando Pirates. Our players such as Ebson Muguyo, Onias Musana, Shadreck Ngwenya and even the mastermind himself George Shaya who trekked down South to seek a fortune and dazzle the crowds with their footwork. So, the return of South Africa was like welcoming a long-lost brother.

The rivalry was strong but there was no animosity, fans looked forward to this encounter. There was no Jomo Sono long considered the crown Prince of South African football, Patrick "Ace" Nsolongoue, Zachariah "Computer" Lamola, there was no Teenage Dladla all popular players in Zimbabwe during their heydays. This fixture had come too late for these greats but in came some new stars and others who were on their last legs. Max "Go man Go" Maponyane was in his thirties but still had something to offer, there were new stars like Fani Madida, Donald "Ace" Khuse, Lucas Radebe, Phillimon

"Chippa" Masinga, captain Neil Tovey and the very popular even among Zimbabwean fans Doctor Khumalo.

On the day of the match, that sun-drenched Sunday afternoon, the National Sports Stadium, our very own Mecca of football,l was packed to the roof. The media in Zimbabwe had done a brilliant job to market the game. The sponsors had come on board, everyone wanted to be part of this Dream. The National coach a master of football mind games deployed the underdog card for Zimbabwe. He made the Ephraim "Screamer" Tshabalala Bafana Bafana strong favourites to win the game. Screamer swallowed the bait, he boasted.

"We are here to play, and we play Shoe Shine Piano!" A new word had entered our football discourse, "Shoe Shine Piano" a football philosophy based on pass and move, a bit of tiki taka with an African flavour. It was a philosophy which the coach did not have too long to implement, he was soon fired after this baptism of fire, but let me not go ahead of the story.

I arrived at the National Sports Stadium early, I wanted to get the best seat. The queues were already building up. Dear reader, have you ever stood in a queue for over an hour without seeming to be making progress? I was losing my patience; many fans were jumping the queue, paying a small token to the guards before being let in. Corruption, well some people never miss an opportunity! A few dollars were made by those manning the gates. The situation was chaotic but good things come to those who wait. Eventually my turn came, and I managed to sneak in just as the teams were warming up. I was relieved! Amazing crowd, flags being waved, the ground a sea of green and yellow. What an atmosphere, what a moment to be Zimbabwean.

The rest as they say is history. South Africa was beaten, not only beaten but given a baptism of fire. They tried to play football, pass and move, pass and move but as we say in terraces "Romance haina mwana.. Kissing and hugging will not lead to a pregnancy ha ha ha!" It is statement which holds true only to those who understand football. Football language! On this day, Zimbabwe won the tactical battle, they picked the moment to attack and they attacked with devastating effect. Bafana Bafana did not know what hit them, they were not humiliated because they put up a good show, there goal was testimony of what their coach believed in, shoe shine piano, but they were shell shocked. Goals win matches and Zimbabwe scored the goals, four to one the scoreboard read.

You must be wondering, what about that goal? Well it was the man we called "Nsunkusonke, The Everyday Wonder," Peter Ndlovu who produced that moment of magic. Adam Ndlovu his elder brother released a pass from deep in his own half. The ball was played into space and Peter using his blistering pace managed to keep the ball in play by the corner flag. Two South African defenders stood before him and the passage to goal. With a sudden burst of speed, he squeezed himself between them leaving the two almost bumping into each other. With the defenders on the deck, he now had to beat the goalkeeper from a tight angle.

What followed next was a moment of magic, an "Ali shuffle" to borrow from "the greatest" in the boxing world, not with his hands but with his feet leaving the keeper grasping thin air with the ball resting calmly in the nets. What a goal, one had to see it to believe it. Simply fantastic and the crowd rose to salute a work of genius.

I was staying in Kuwadzana, about ten kilometres from the National Sports Stadium. I did not bother to find a lift back home. I simply joined the mass of bodies trekking back home on feet. Everyone was trying to explain to anyone who cared to listen the events that led to that goal.

"He did this," one would say. "No, he did this."

Every imitation was a better version of the last one and everyone was convinced that theirs was the best. In Kuwadzana's Blue Fountain Bar, where we settled for refreshments after the long walk, the conversations continued and with each sip of the frothy brew, the tale of the goal began to grow wings. To this day, the goal is still regarded as one of the best scored at the National Sports Stadium. It will always be cherished. It was a goal which left the Bafana Bafana defenders shell shocked. It was a goal which made us dream!

I must admit that I jumped the gun in my narration of the National Team experiences, but I had to begin with the highlight. Lest we forget, soon after independence in 1980, Zimbabwe was welcomed back into the international sporting arena. Before 1980, we were in isolation because of the racist policies of the Rhodesia government. With the white supremacist government now in the dustbin of history the international sporting doors were opened. To celebrate this readmission, we invited our friends Zambia, Mozambique and Malawi. It was the new nation's first test of international football and the players did not disappoint. The first group of players such as Raphael Phiri, Graham Boyle, Sunday Marimo, Oliver Kateya, Misheck Marimo, Ephert Lungu, Wonder Phiri, Joseph Zulu, Robert Godoka, Max Tshuma, Shacky Tauro, David Muchineripi, Rodrick Simwanza among others with John Rugg were the pioneers of this international journey.

The first taste of international glory came in 1985, and this was the Confederation of East and Central Africa Football Association trophy (CECAFA) when Zimbabwe beat Kenya by two goals to one at Rufaro Stadium. It was a triumph of football development because the players had been together for over five years. The core of the team which won the trophy had played together in the Under 20 team in 1980 and five years later they lifted the nation's first notable trophy.

Players like Japhet Mparutsa, James Takavada David Mwanza, Stanley Ndunduma, Joel Shambo, Edward Katsvere, David Zulu, Ephraim Dzimbiri among others had started together on this football journey. Others came later like Moses Chunga and Gift Mpariwa. There were some senior players like Misheck Marimo, Ephert Lungu, Oliver Kateya, Joseph Zulu, a perfect mix and they delivered.

Many African nations played against Zimbabwe in World Cup and Africa Nations cup games and even friendly matches. Some great football powerhouses such as Cameroon, Algeria and Egypt had some great players. This allowed our players, The Warriors as we now called the National players an opportunity to rub shoulders with the best. They played with such greats as Ali Feghani, Ali Shehata, Raber Madjer and yes Jean Betrand Bocande. It is to Bocande that I now dedicate the next two paragraphs. He deserves it.

On 18 August 1985, Zimbabwe Warriors played Senegal nicknamed "The Teranga Lions" in a World Cup qualifier. Rufaro Stadium, the venue of the match, was packed to the roof. News had filtered through that Bocande, the deadly dreadlocked striker who was banging goals in France at a time when African players were very few in Europe, was in the team and everyone wanted to see the legend for themselves. However, when the teams trotted out, Bocande was not in the team. Apparently, he had never bothered to travel from his base in France. He trusted his teammates to roll past us.

Zimbabwe had not read the script; they came out fighting and scored a sensational one to nil victory. The Senegalese had to save the match in the return league in two weeks time, and that is when the story of Bocande really begins.

One September 1985, Dakar, sweltering heat, packed stadium, the crowd baying for blood, the Warriors

103

rolled into the Stade Leopold Sedar Senghor National Stadium for the battle of their lives. Senegal did not take any chances. It was a must-win match, so they chartered a special plane for their deadly marksman, Jean Betrand Bocande. He arrived some thirty minutes before the match and was rushed to the stadium.

"The crowd went into a frenzy, we were already at the stadium and we realised that he had arrived!" said Japhet 'Shortcat' Mparutsa who was in goals for the Warriors on that fateful day.

"We are dying here in the 36 degrees of Dakar, that man Bocande is cutting through the Warriors defence like a hot knife through butter!"

The man tasked to bring the action for us from Dakar, Evans Mambara, screamed as we listened on our radios. The whole Nation was glued to the radio and we could feel the pain.

"Bocande, Bocande Bocande, we are in trouble here, 10000 kilometres away from home, we are dead and buried!" screamed dear Evans. His pain was real. He loved the Warriors. The Warriors were being mauled by the Lions of Teranga. They were dying a slow death in the heat of Dakar and Bocande was plunging one dagger after another into their hearts.

He scored a hatrick! Yes, to borrow from our commentator of the day, we were dead and buried! The gulf in class between Bocande and our best defenders had been cruelly exposed. The legend had shown why he was the French League's top goal scorer that season. He taught us a football lesson.

After such humiliation, an introspection was needed. Wislow Graboswiki, the coach, was not happy with the defending. He was furious with Misheck Marimo and Ernest Mutano – his two centre backs for failing to contain Bocande. He bought a newspaper the following morning and it confirmed his feelings. Bocande was jumping up scoring a header unmarked.

"Where were you kurwa, show me where were you?" he asked; his face all red. He was fond of that word kurwa which was pronounced as "kruvha" a Polish swear word and used it when he was angry. Ernest Mutano was called "Mr Cool" for never panicking under pressure when he was on the pitch and his answer here showed why he deserved that moniker off the pitch as well.

"I was there, the cameraman just missed me!" He said nonchalantly, to bursts of laughter from the team.

"This diffused the tense situation which was threatening to explode and even the angry coach just laughed," said Japhet Mparutsa – the narrator of these events in a later interview.

Indeed, Bocande had left a trail of destruction and dear reader you can appreciate why I have dedicated these paragraphs to this legend. He is a man whom we still talk about some thirty years later. Many young players at grassroots started calling themselves Bocande, he had that impact on our collective memory.

But we had to move on from this morale sapping defeat. When we played Congo Brazzaville National Sports Stadium on 14 July 1991, we had healed. We had high hopes as a nation, to qualify for Senegal in 1992. The team was strong with several foreign based internationals like Moses Chunga who was in Belgium, Willard Khumalo and Henry Mackop who playing for lower league clubs in Germany. The combination between mercurial captain Moses Chunga and rising star Peter Ndlovu had shown a lot of promise. Fans were confident, and the team seemed to be cruising racing to a two to nil lead. Then Congo Brazzaville pulled one back, a mere consolation we thought. Then the moment when the whole Nation cried arrived! A hopeful punt up field and everyone expected goalkeeper John Sibanda to make a routine save. Fate intervened, or was it a curse? John Sibanda dropped the ball into his own net.

The National Sports Stadium resembled a deserted cemetery, it was the silence of the dead. The whole nation was united in grief and John Sibanda became the most hated figure in Zimbabwe football. Up to now many have not forgiven him! Willard Khumalo, the Zimbabwe midfield kingpin summed it all about poor John's tragic moment "I saw fear in his eyes!" Indeed, it must have been fear which made him commit that schoolboy error. It took us a while to recover from such psychological wound inflicted by one of our own.

In the end we recovered just in time to begin a new journey with renewed hope. The Dream Team as the Zimbabwe National team were now known, came to the fore and our hopes were raised again. This team embarked on a journey which nearly took the nation to Tunisia Afcon 1994 and USA World Cup 94. On both journeys, we were close, very close but again we fell on the last hurdle. Let me talk about the good times first.

Reinard Fabisch came to Zimbabwe on a government exchange programme from Germany, liked what he saw, stayed on, married one of our own and took the Nation on a football dream journey. He promoted several young players from the under 23 team and mixed them with some senior players. What came out was a formidable outfit which made waves throughout Africa. Fabisch also brought the man known globally as "The Jungleman" Bruce Grobelaar.

Everyone was excited, they came on board including the white and Asian fans who had long deserted the game. This made the giant National Sports Stadium a true reflection of the Zimbabwe society in all its diversity. The cooperate world came to the fore and there were positive vibes all over and boy did the team deliver great results! The team went on a thirteen-match unbeaten run, Egypt,

Cameroon, Angola, Togo, Zambia, Guinea all came and fell by the wayside. The National Stadium known by its moniker as "PaGomba," became a burial ground for some of the best teams in Africa. We even took the battle to Lyon against Egypt and managed to get a draw. It was a history-breaking run until Kalusha came to town with what looked like a depleted Zambian team.

Zambia had lost an entire squad off the coast of Gabon, a tragedy which broke the hearts of all football lovers. It was the crème de la crème of Zambian football, Richard Mwanza, Efford Chabala, John Soko, Whiteson Changwe, Robert Watiyakeni, Winter Mumba, Eston Mulenga, Samuel Chomba, Kenan Simambe, Derby Makinka, Derby Makinka, Moses Chikwalakwala, Wisdom Chansa, Numba Mwila, Godfery Kangwa, Patrice Banda, Kevin Mutale, Timothy Mwitwa, Moses Masuwa, coaches Alex Chola and Godfrey Ucar Chitalu, a golden generation wiped out on that fateful day on 28 April 1993.

We mourned them, they were our brothers, we knew them, they were our heroes too, but the match had to go ahead. When Zambia came, they looked like a beaten team but Kalusha had other ideas. With nine minutes to go, he stole in to flick a header past the Jungleman in goals for Zimbabwe. One could hear the drop of a pin in the giant Stadium, another heartbreak. I could not sleep for weeks, I was haunted by this result, we were nine minutes away from qualifying for our very first Africa Cup of Nations tournament. We had the team but bottled it, I was heartbroken.

The team then went to Cameroon needing a win to qualify for World cup USA 94 and lost three to one amid accusation of bribery and match fixing. A campaign which had promised so much ended up with nothing to show for it. We asked again, "Are we a cursed Nation?". It felt like that that until Mhofu Sunday Marimo came along. The good times rolled again.

When Mhofu was appointed he came on a seemingly impossible mission, like many before him. We used to sing in our churches "Ndorikwira sei gomo, rine minzwa inobaya, pfugama unamate. How can I overcome this hurdle, kneel down and pray!" Indeed, after so many near misses and heartbreaks, all we could do as a Nation was to pray for Divine intervention. We prayed for Mhofu to overcome this hurdle. The man himself was confident, in one interview he later said "I gathered the players together and said, listen, we know the problems in our country, we know the problems with Zifa and money but let us focus on the football. Let us make history, let us qualify for Tunisia 2004. "

It turned out to be an inspired speech. When the campaign was launched with a match against Mali on the 8th of September 2002, the team delivered a solid performance. I attended this match and the confidence cascaded from the fans to the players. Lazarus Muhoni earned his nickname "Mali" by scoring the only goal. By the end of the campaign, history had been made, results went in our favour and the whole nation celebrated. The curse which many of us thought had been pronounced by Ben Koufie, "Even if you hire a coach from the moon, you will never qualify", had been broken. Did he curse us? Now we did not care, the monkey was off our back as a nation. "Tunisia, here come!" we cried in unison.

We went, we saw, we did not exactly conquer. We won one match and lost two, we returned home early. But we had some memorable moments like Esrom Nyandoro's thunderous shot against Cameroon which was voted as one of the goals of the tournament. What about the gazelle like run of Joel Lupaphla before he scored against Algeria. Those were beautiful moments but there were horrible ones too. Like the now infamous" Mugeyi miss!", the moment when Wilfred Mugeyi wished the earth could open up and swallow him. He missed an open goal; it is a miss that will follow him to the grave. "The Mugeyi Miss" became the butt of jokes. It is embedded in Zimbabwe football folklore.

We were beaten but not humiliated. Sunday Chidzambwa and his team came back to a 'heroes' welcome. Many had tried and failed but a local coach had done it. Once the hoodoo had been broken, three more qualifications were achieved all by local coaches. Charles Mhaluri and Callisto Pasuwa and then Chidzambwa again made the qualification to the Nations Cup routine.

The challenges for these coaches during the qualification process were the same, lack of adequate preparations, no friendly matches, broken promises on bonuses and many other challenges. There were boycotts and strikes by the players and despite all this the coaches soldiered on. Although respective teams have failed to go beyond the second round of the Afcon tournaments that we have been to, I respect what the coaches have done. There is need to make the next step up and go further when we qualify but for a nation which has experienced economic meltdown since the year 2000 this has been a remarkable achievement. Football has been a shining light despite the doom and gloom, it has put smiles on many of us.

Another success story at National Level was with the junior teams especially at Under 23 level. The under Under 20 team which was assembled in 1980 was one of the strongest and had Japhet Mparutsa, Lucky Dube, JamesTakavada, Ephriam Dzimbiri, Sabastine Chikwature, David Mwanza, Stanley Ndunduma, Joel Shambo, Madinda Ndlovu, Rainos Mapfumo, Anderson Maposa and Zachariah Chironda among other future stars. Most of these players went on to represent Zimbabwe Senior team. The same can be said about the 1990 under 23 team which had the likes of Peter Ndlovu, Adam Ndlovu,

Benjamin Nkonjera and Agent Sawu who also became full internationals.

In 1995 we also had a very strong under 23 squad which nearly qualified for the Atlanta 1996 Olympics only for them to fall at the last hurdle against eventual gold medalists Nigeria. Our team had the likes of Muzondiwa Mugadza, Butler Masango, Alois Bunjira, Vusi Laher, George Mbwando, Methembe Ndlovu, Cain and Abel Muteji and Stuart Murisa. There were a bunch of really good players who gave us so much hope. Sadly, we seem to have abandoned this well-structured development strategy and we have not had strong junior teams emerging in recent years. Zifa the mother body should have a rethink and priotirise once more the junior teams.

A narrative on our National Team cannot be complete without mentioning the tragedies that befell us. When Alec Fidesi, Eularia Made, T. Makonese, Tawanda Gwanzura, Patrick Mpariwa, Killian Madondo, George Chin'anga, Sam Mavhuro, Enock Chimombe, Joyce Chimbamba, Nenhilda Magadu, Ronald Kufakunesu and Tonderai Jeke joined the thousands of Zimbabwe fans who thronged the National Sports Stadium, it looked like a normal sporting outing despite the high stakes of the match.

The Warriors were going to do battle with perennial rivals Bafana Bafana in a World cup qualifier on 9 september 2000. What had started as a normal day became tragic when the police overacted and threw teargas into the crowd. A few disgruntled fans had thrown missiles onto the pitch when Bafana Bafana scored their third goal.

The law and order authorities instead of managing the situation better, in their wisdom or lack of it threw teargas into the packed stands causing a stampede. With that stampede, the thirteen fans lost their lives and families were torn apart. This was an avoidable tragedy in my view, these fans should never have lost their lives, the police overreacted. As a nation, we will always remember these fallen heroes.

Nineteen years later, on 23 March 2019, another tragedy happened at the bowl-shaped stadium. Although the magnitude was of a low scale, every life matters so allow me to mourn Egna Nyamadzawo who was crushed by a gate as she tried to enter the stadium. It was a unfortunate accident which brought to the fore the topic of fans safety at our National stadiums. The lady is a football hero, she died in the line of duty leaving behind two children and a distraught husband who watched her being crushed to death. Heartbreaking!

The National team was also tarnished by match fixing scandals which became known as the Asiagate Scandal. Respected journalists, coaches and players were accused of fixing matches. When matches are fixed, the integrity of football is brought into disrepute. About eighty players and officials were accused of accepting bribes to throw away matches between 2007 and 2009. Matches were arranged in far away nations like Malaysia, Vietnam and Thailand for betting purposes.

The players, coaches and journalists were found guilty, suspended, banned and ostracised in society. In the end the suspensions were lifted but the damage on the image of the National Team and on the people responsible was indelible. They will live with it, a black stain on their characters. Many still protest their innocence but in the minds of the fans, they remain guilty as charged. A lot of trust and good will was lost. How unfortunate!

However, apart from the National team, our clubs also gave us some memorable moments. Africa is blessed with some great clubs and some of them visited Zimbabwe. From 1980 onwards, our clubs were now able to compete with the champions in other African leagues. Early visitors included such powerhouses as Lupopo

Football Club of Zaire, Shooting Stars of Nigeria, Kampala City Council of Uganda and Jet of Algeria. All these teams left an indelible mark on our football terrain.

I remember when Dynamos Football Club played Shooting Stars in 1982. The first leg was in Nigeria and the media wrote off Dynamos "Visiting the Lion's den...Sheep being led to the slaughter" were some of the headlines which were churned out by the media in Nigeria. Dynamos Football club refused to be intimidated, they wrote their own narrative and came out fighting. They conjured up an improbable two to one win. This result sent shock waves throughout Africa and more was to come. If the Nigerians thought that this was a fluke, they had not seen anything yet. The match in Harare will be remembered for the scintillating performance of Edward Katsvere. He gave the Nigerians a torrid time as Dynamos hammered the giants by three goals to nil. I am sure on their way back, the Nigerians had one name in their conversation, Edward Katsvere, what a blinder he played on this day!

Other teams were also humiliated like Dinamo Di Fima of Madagascar. They were massacred by Caps United in an Africa Cup Winners fixture, but they left us with the nickname Dynamos De Mbare. Our creative fans quickly appropriated the name and fine tuned it to rhyme with Dynamos so the most popular club in the country became Dynamos De Mbare. From a humiliating defeat, a new name was born, and that name endures up to this day.

Other exciting teams like Zamalek, Lupopo, Arab Contractors, Gor Mahia, Maji Maji, ASEC Mimosas, Accra Hearts of Oak, Cotton Sport among others also came, some were massacred but others broke our hearts. Some names were so exciting to the extent that some drinking places were named after them. ASEC Mimosas, a drinking hole in Kuwadzana 5 became known as PaMimosa. As a Caps United fan, I will never forget the four to nil thrashing that the team suffered at the hands of AFC Leopards of Kenya.

"AFC MAUL CAPS UNITED," was the screaming headline and yes it was a mauling. I still remember Wilberforce Mulamba, the man who did the damage. It happened in 1988 but for me, it seems like yesterday, a genuine supporter does not forget these matches. It was also the first match in which the " Headmaster" himself, Joel Shambo was substituted. It was a humiliation for both club and captain. As we say in street football lingo "Football can kill you indeed."

Two clubs however deserve special praise for the way they represented the motherland on the African Safari, Blackpool and Dynamos. Blackpool reached the semi final of the Cup Winners Cup in 1996 while Dynamos reached the final of the Champions League final in 1998.

Blackpool, the flamboyant outfit owned by Directors Gorden Chadamunhu, Joe Salifu, Joe "Pajero" Masenda, Ginger Chinguwa, Ben Muchedzi, Lecture Mpanje, Ronnie Chihota and Forbes Mutawa embarked on an enthralling journey which grabbed the attention of all and sundry and shook the corridors of African football power in 1996..

Powered by the goals of George "Zambia" Mbwando and Hubert Munjanja the indefatigable Masimba Dinyero in midfield with Collins Kabote, Clifton Kadurira, Vincent Chigaga, Caany Tongesayi, big Joseph Dube, Simba Nyakudziwanza, Vusi Laher among others providing the spine of the team. They were expertly guided by the charismatic Joel Shambo, aided by former teammates Shacky Tauro and Friday Phiri.

They claimed some big scalps and pencil slim striker George Mbwando earned his nickname "Zambia" during this campaign. He played so well against Zambia club Kabwe Warriors scoring both goals away from home that the fans came up with the nickname. Of course having played well against Zambia Under 23 when he again scored

113

also enhanced his reputation and gave strength to the nickname. The Cup Winners Cup campaign changed the course of his life as he soon earned a move to Germany with Bonner SC. However, against JS Kabyile of Algeria, the semi final proved to be one battle too many. They succumbed to a two to one defeat in Algeria having won the first leg one nil in Harare. The away goal rule knocked them out but the whole of Africa had noticed. It was a heroic performance.

Then came Dynamos who were not the strongest but who had a togetherness which carried them all the way to the final in 1998. The team leapt over improbable hurdles, promises were made to the players, promises were broken, players boycotted training, players were suspended but this team still bounced back. It had nine lives like the proverbial cat, the team refused to give up the ghost ! They reached the final of Africa most prestigious club competition. What a remarkable achievement.

There were many heroes in this campaign including some who fell by the wayside like George Mandizvidza. When Dynamos played Ferroviaria of Mozambique for a place in the knockout stages, George Mandizvidza produced a save which has gone down in Zimbabwe football history as one of the best made by a local goalkeeper. It was a gravity defying save, he changed direction in mid air to tip the ball over the bar and this made the Mozambique fans believe that he was using the dark arts of juju. They tried to grab his cap and gloves bag to weaken this perceived juju.

However, it was not juju, just a moment of brilliance which catapulted Dynamos into the next round. Unfortunately, that was to be his final contribution to the journey since he was suspended soon after complaining abaout the lack of bonuses. In the group stages, Dynamos topped a strong group which had African giants Accra

Hearts of Oak, ES Sahel and Eagle Cement to reach the final where they faced Asec Mimmossa of Ivory Coast.

In the final, tragedy struck, Captain Memory Mucherahowa was head butted during the warm up and nearly died on the pitch. Without their influential captain, Dynamos were rudderless and lost the match by four goals to two. It was another of those so near and yet so far familiar Zimbabwe football stories. Coach Sunday Chidzambwa and his group of dedicated warriors became instant heroes. Their story will forever be remembered!

But it will be amiss not mention the familiar Dynamos story of promises, broken promises and betrayal. Captain Memory Mucherahova said, "I nearly died in Ivory Coast, the clubs' bosses promised us that this tournament was going to change our lives. We expected big financial rewards but instead they shifted the goal posts and accused some of our players of selling the match. It was unbelievable and at that moment I realised that our struggle had been in vain," he said in his autobiography. For those fans who are familiar with this team, there are no surprises, it is the modus operandi of those who have run the club over the years. Players welfare is the last thing on their list of priorities. I call it the ultimate betrayal!

The African safari for both country and clubs had many cherished moments. It had its highs and lows, but all this contributed to the journey into fandom that this book seeks to capture. I hope I have done justice to that.

And yes, one of the most enduring statements ever made on the local scene was said by a disgruntled captain of the National team. Moses Chunga fed up with the poor bonuses offered by the authorities declared, "I do not play for peanuts!" It is a statement which still resonates with the current generation of players. The National team journey it is often spiced and replete with endless challenges, but the good moments shine through too.

These will always be cherished and the coaches and players who contributed to the journey will always have my respect!

Chapter 9
Football rivalries: Zimbabwe is no exception!

"Caps United Hammer Dynamos for Seven!" was the screaming headline in the country's top selling newspaper – The Herald one Monday morning in 1987. That headline is regarded as one of the most iconic ever written by sports journalist Sam Marisa, a headline which captured the humiliation of the " seven million club" Dynamos by eternal rivals Caps United in a National Foods Africa Day semi final at Rufaro Stadium. The joke was on Dynamos, as Caps United fans celebrated the rout, "A goal for every million!" they taunted .

As Caps United fans, we rubbed it in for the blue half of the country. This result remains a rich deposit in the memory bank of all Caps United fans. The defeat hurt the Dynamos fans, it was victory which Caps United fans never miss an opportunity to remind them of. It was a result which cemented the rivalry between the popular clubs. There are many such rivalries in the Zimbabwe football narrative and it is to these that I dedicate this chapter on my football experience!

The world over, football rivalries are the oxygen which give life to most football leagues. Football fans love rivalries, the players are aware of them and teams try not to lose against their sworn enemies. Think of Barcelona versus Real Madrid, AC Milan versus Inter Milan, Celtic against Rangers, Arsenal and Tottenham, Kaizer Chiefs versus Orlando Pirates popular known as the Soweto derby and one of the fiercest in the world Boca Juniors against River Plate.

The reason for the rivalries make the study of sport as an academic enterprise such a fascinating area. The reasons range from the petty like Inter Milan disagreeing with AC Milan about whether to sign foreign players or not, to the deep seated irreconcilable differences for example religion as in the case of Celtic against Rangers. Sometimes the rivalries can be toxic, and it is then that football becomes the ugly sport. In Africa we have a fair share of rivalries too, Alhy against Zamalek, Gor Mahia against AFC Leopards, Kaiser Chiefs versus Orlando Pirates but let me focus on Zimbabwe because we do not have a shortage of these.

In 1981, I fell in love with Caps United and the fixture that I looked forward to most was the one against Dynamos. In Harare on match day, the city was and is divided into two, the green half and the blue half, the colours of the two rivals. Dynamos call themselves the "Pride of Zimbabwe", have always had the numbers both in terms of titles and the fan base while Caps United pride themselves as "The Cup Kings" Dynamos Football Club boast that they have seven million supporters. Caps United were like the stubborn young brother seeking to knock the big brother from his established perch. Nothing satisfied the Caps United fans more than to give Dynamos that knockout punch and any victory was celebrated with gusto.

The same applied to Dynamos fans, they hated and still hate to lose against football upstarts as they view Caps United. This fixture dominated discussions before and after it had been played, it is a fixture which created heroes and endeared many in the hearts of fans. The fixture became a reference point for many football conversations, "Do you remember that day when Gift Mudangwe destroyed Dynamos or Do you remember that day when Moses Chunga terrorised the Caps United defence," fans are fond of saying.

The seven-nil drubbing of Dynamos by Caps United will live long in the memory of any Zimbabwe football fan.

It was a chastening experience for the "Boys in Blue". Caps United with the man we called the Headmaster, Joel "Jubilee" Shambo also known by others as "Mwalimu," Swahili for Teacher in full flow humiliated Dynamos at their favourite hunting ground Rufaro Stadium. On a bright Sunday afternoon, the Dynamos players wished that the ground would open up and swallow them. Erick Aisam the makeshift Dynamos right back had a torrid time against an on fire Shacky Tauro.

Tauro the lethal Caps United striker buried four goals past Dynamos a feat he should have enjoyed because he genuinely loved to play beat Dynamos. Tauro totally destroyed the then young defender Eric Aisam who had been drafted in as a makeshift right back. It was a baptism of fire. The man who did the damage however was none other than Joel Shambo. Sam Marisa captured it well in describing Shambo 's contribution to the game. He wrote, "Shambo, affectionately called "The Headmaster" lived up to his nickname as he made Dynamos midfielders look like his pupils. Shambo was instrumental in Caps United's first, second, third, sixth and seventh goals."

Dear reader, this was a perfect midfield display by the legendary midfielder. It was such performances which made me fall in love with this man, which made me declare myself a "Shamboist", a self created term which is simply a tribute to the ball skills and creative artistry of this maestro. What a match this was and what a performance by the boys in green. The Dynamos fans simply hate to be reminded of this dark day in the history of their great club, but history does not lie, they just must live with it.

Dynamos did make amends in another match in a Chibuku trophy semi final hammering Caps United by six goals to two. This gave the Dynamos fans a measure of satisfaction; a bit of pride was restored. This was the match when two senior players exchanged blows on the pitch resulting in both being shown the red card. Shacky

Tauro hated to lose against Dynamos and Misheck "Scania" Marimo, the Dynamos captain knew about this very well. He never missed the chance to taunt him and rubbed it in by ruffling Tauro's long Afro hair. This habit, Shacky hated with a passion and on this day, he lost it! Boom, a blow landed on Misheck's mouth. Misheck was a giant of a man and his reaction to this was predictable.

Tauro found himself lying on the turf, knocked out by a hard one from the towering defender. The referee flashed his mandatory red card, he did not have a choice. It was a day of shame for the two great players as they were forced to take an early shower, but it showed the intense rivalry.

This rivalry has produced many heroes. It has also produced villains. Heroes such as Archford "Chehuchi" Chimutanda who in the 1982 derby scored a goal of such quality that the fans who witnessed it still talk about it to this day. It was one of those Chimutanda Magic moments! On this big occasion, the Rothmans Trophy final, he overran the Caps United midfield department which had Stix Mtizwa and Joel Shambo in the mix. This was no mean feat since the two were regarded as the best midfielders of their generation.

Another battle which always fascinated fans was that between Stanley Ndunduma of Caps United on the right wing against attacking left back Oliver Kateya of Dynamos. Every time this fixture came around, fans were assured of drama as the gifted Ndunduma tried to outwit the hard running Kateya. It was difficult to tell who would come out on top but there was entertainment galore.

Another genius, Moses Chunga delivered some mesmerising performances for Dynamos. Legend has it that Duncan Ellison the Caps united goalkeeper used to shout at his defenders "Makai Moze... mark Moze!", he learnt Shona just to give this instruction.

What about Gift Mudangwe who in one game under floodlights ran the Dynamos defence ragged that the Herald Sports Editor Jahor Omar wrote, "Gift Mudangwe might not be a household name in the Zimbabwe sports fraternity, but ask any Dynamos fan who watched the match yesterday, they will now know him!" Gift Mudangwe had announced himself on the big stage with a bang and left a trail of destruction among the Dynamos ranks.

Yes, I also watched a young Masimba Mbuwa score a Marco Van Bastenlike goal to claim victory for Dynamos at Gwanzura Stadium. Sadly, for the upcoming star, it was to be his last notable contribution to the Dynamos cause. But for that flirting moment, he was a hero for the legion of fans who follow Dynamos. They expected more, but more did not come, his loss of form was a mystery. Dear reader, there was also Never "Maswera sei" Chiku. He always rose from the bench for Caps United to score the winner usually with his head against Dynamos. He was the Dynamos nemesis, the player whom Dynamos fans hated to see warming up. They knew trouble was coming and indeed, he caused trouble.

Alois Bunjira, Stewart Murisa, Morgan Nkathazo for Caps United, Tauya Murewa, Bhekhi Mlotshwa, Simon Chuma for Dynamos all delivered some unforgettable moments for their respective teams. Joe Mugabe and Memory Mucherahova were the best of friends off the pitch but bitter rivals on it. Once they donned the respective team colours, all friendship was forgotten. What a battle these two engaged in the middle of the park, the battle for midfield dominance.

There were villains too, like the day that Dynamos goalkeeper dropped a harmless looking cross into his own nets. It was a howler which was to define his career at Dynamos. The rivalry also brought out the worst among the fans with acts of hooliganism often leading to the abandonment of matches. When I embarked on this football journey in the 1980s, the rivalry among the fans was intense but not toxic or violent. It was more of banter and fans used to sit together in the stands.

In the 90's however, the rivalry became violent, many fans came into the game who created mayhem on match days. As a result, matches were abandoned or if not abandoned, fans were beaten up, especially when Dynamos lost. This was unfortunate because this rivalry should be about football not about spreading violence. Unfortunately, there were some who were hell bent on causing mayhem and often, this grabbed the headlines at the expense of the football. I am glad that there are some supporters like Chris Musekiwa, well known as Romario who have tried to encourage peace among the rival supporters. Currently cases of violence among the rival fans is at a minimum. Long may it continue, we can be rivals but the football must win in the end.

Another prominent rivalry is that between Dynamos versus Highlanders. This has attracted the attention of academics who have sought to unravel what lies at the heart of this football rivalry. Both Dynamos and Highlanders are great clubs, they are more than clubs in the eyes of their fans and they reside deep in the hearts of their supporters. The rival between the two is often depicted as the "Battle for Zimbabwe," it is a struggle for the domination of Zimbabwe Football. I accept that the two clubs are the oxygen that Zimbabwe football needs. When the two clubs play well, there is no better football carnival in Zimbabwe, the sea of blue at Rufaro, the mixture of black and white at Barbourfields stadium, dear reader those are sights to behold.

Highlanders call themselves "Ithimu yelizwe lonke" the country's team, while Dynamos call themselves the "Seven Million Club" because they claim to have that number of supporters, which at one point was the entire population of Zimbabwe. If one adds the tribal element to the mix, with Bosso having a predominant Ndebele fan base and Dynamos dominating among the Shona, this rivalry becomes very intense and can become toxic.

There is a pride in these two dominant Zimbabwe tribes and this is often expressed through the football. Our country has gone through unfortunate political upheavals from the pre-colonial to the post independence era which have often shaped how these two tribes view each other. The memories of the tragic period of Gukurahundi in the early years of independence, a period many in Matebeleland view as ethnic cleansing or genocide still linger on. Football can be used as an outlet to vent frustrations against the government. For many who support Highlanders, the team is more than a football club. It is a cultural institution and football victories over Dynamos are cherished. When results do not come however, violence becomes an option. Yes, some have sought to advance their supremacist and separatist ideas through the two clubs and with such characters, the football can take a back seat.

Fortunately, the football has often triumphed over whatever agendas that some might have. So, to football let us pay tribute. Heroes have emerged from both sides of the football divide. In the 80's it was the likes of Peter Nkomo, Mecedes Sibanda, Willard Khumalo, Titus Majola, Nhamo Shambira, Tobias Mudyambanje, Tanny Banda, Madinda, Adam and later Peter Ndlovu from Bosso as Highlanders are known by their loyal fans who gave us some unforgettable moments.

Dynamos have had great players too like Moses Chunga, Edward Katsvere, Kateya, Mandigora later Tauya Murehwa, Vitalis Takawira and Memory Mucherahova. The names are too numerous to mention. The rivalry continues up to this day, but it is not as intense as it used to be, the quality of players has gone down. However, any match between Dynamos and Highlanders always attract a full house, there were packed stadiums in the 80's, there are still packed stadiums to this day. Dynamos against Highlanders, was the match then. It remains the match in Zimbabwe football. The match remains the oxygen that Zimbabwe football needs, I say "Long Live" to what the media have called "The Battle of Zimbabwe".

Another rivalry which was also toxic was the Zimbabwe Saints against Highlanders one. The tribal dimension was well pronounced in this and the political leaders had to intervene to reduce the tension. Both clubs claim the second city Bulawayo as their roots, but the tribal separation was notable in their initial names with Zimbabwe Saints being called Mashonaland United and Highlanders called Matebeleland Highlanders. Inevitably the Shona people who were settled in Bulawayo were more inclined towards the former while the Ndebele people supported the later.

Politicians such as the late Vice President Joshua Nkomo and former Health Minister Herbet Ushehwekunze persuaded the teams to drop the tribal terms and so Mashonaland United became Zimbabwe Saints in 1977 and Matebeleland became just Highlanders. Did this help? I am not sure, but I spoke to a man who lived through this rivalry as a coach but had brothers on both sides of the football divide, Tendai Chieza, the 1970 Soccer Star of the year.

He had this to say, "The atmosphere before matches was poisonous, the week after the matches was even worse, my brother Itai and Winston were at Bosso, myself and George were at Zimbabwe Saints, a week before the match we did not speak, the week after the match we were like strangers! Football, the beautiful game was keeping us apart!"

Yes, the rivalry was intense, but football is a powerful sport and football triumphed over all adversity. Great matches were played when these two giants were in the then Super League and later in the Zimbabwe Premier Soccer league. From the days of Ebson "Sugar" Muguyo, Chita Antonio, Musa Muzanenhamo, Onias Musana, Max "Shaluza" Tshuma, Andrew Kadengu, William Sibanda to the later years of Ephraim Chawanda, Joseph Machingura, Obey Sova, Norman Gumbo among others, Zimbabwe Saints have always produced quality players. These pitted their skills against the Highlanders greats of each given era, from the likes of Douglas "British" Mloyi to later generation of Willard Khumalo, Peter Ndlovu and Benjamin Nkonjera among others.

Barbourfields Stadium was the arena of these battles. Some scintillating performances were witnessed and the residents of the city of Kings Bulawayo were spoiled. It is such a shame that Zimbabwe Saints fell victim to the endless power struggles among its leaders and now languishes in the lower echelons of Zimbabwe Football. This deprived the premier league of one of the strongest football rivalry ever to emerge. Cry the beloved Zimbabwe Saints, "Chauya Chikwata!"

Other rivalries have come and gone, like Gweru United against Bata Power. This divided the city of Gweru. It was a proper derby, but it has become extinct, both Gweru United and Bata Power are now a distant memory, existing only in the minds of those lucky enough to have been born when the teams existed.

Amazulu Football club owned by businessman Delma Lupepe came carrying with it the "Galactico" tag. They were flamboyant and recruited players from city rivals Highlanders and Zimbabwe Saints. The fans of both clubs hated them because they flashed the money and when they grabbed the Championship from Highlanders who had been on a run of four consecutive titles, they became a direct rival.

The rivalry was however short lived, the owner Delma Lupepe was unable to sustain the project. Religious convictions also interfered with the fulfilment of fixtures. The owner being a Seventh Day Adventist, did not want his team to play on a Saturday and when other clubs refused to budge, he decided to disband the team.

A statement which will resonate long in the history of Zimbabwe football was made by the team's manager Felix Matsika in announcing the decision. He said, "If we have to chose between the Sabbath and football, we will choose the Sabbath. Football laws are made by man, but the Sabbath was written by the finger of God." With that bold statement, the fate of the flamboyant Amazulu Football Club was sealed. It was a triumph of conviction over football, Heavenly principles over man-made rules and Zimbabwe football was left in a poorer state.

Moneybags, as they are called Platinum Football Club, came to the fore and took the Zimbabwe football fraternity by storm. They grabbed the limelight from Highlanders, Dynamos and Caps United and they have since won three titles on the trot from 2017 to 2019.

Rich as they are by Zimbabwe standards, they have poor neighbours who always gave them a run for their money before they were relegated from the league. Shabanie Mine Footbal Club. This is a football club that lit the league when the going was good. But the harsh economic challenges forced the club on its knees. They were reduced to paupers, but even in that state, their matches against their rich neighbours remained fierce. This was a rival to match any other that emerged from the Zimbabwe league. It is a shame that it is no more, a victim of the harsh environmental conditions.

Indeed, my journey into football fandom was inspired by many of these derbies and football rivalries. Like thousands of other fans, I looked forward to Dynamos versus Caps United, Highlanders against Dynamos, Caps United playing against Black Aces among others.

Many heroes emerged from these matches, players earned nicknames by simply performing well. A story is told of how Andrew Kadengu the skilful Zimbabwe Saints winger earned his nickname "Mai Maria." Apparently on one Sunday before a match against city rivals Highlanders, he went to church. Some fans saw him coming out church and when he scored a goal in the afternoon, the the religious nickname "Mai Maria" stuck with him. It was creative on the part of the fans as well as a fitting tribute to the man with an angelic face but a lethal left foot. There are many such stories woven around these encounters.

It will be amiss not to also talk about the various mind games which surround these games, tales of juju, tales of n'angas or traditional healers employed by teams and paid loads of money, tales of rituals which had to be performed to win games. Urine is a big part of these practices with ball boys being instructed to pour it at goalposts. Although these rituals can happen even in ordinary games, it is with rivals that such practices reach unprecedented levels.

Other rituals included waiting for your rival to get onto the pitch first and matches were often delayed as teams argued on who should be first. Sometimes teams refused to use the dressing rooms, wary of the juju and at times they scaled fences to get onto the pitch to avoid the power of juju at official entrances. Sometimes the beliefs became ridiculous like the case of former Dynamos goalkeeper Tendai Tanyanyiwa who made a startling confession on his Face book page.

"A certain Chairman always asked me to look at his bare bottom, this was meant to bring me luck as I kept goal. Every time we won without conceding a goal, he took credit for the result, thanking his bottom baring antics! The football world can be a crazy world indeed," wrote Tanyanyiwa. I have quoted him verbatim on this one. All this was all part of the strong desire not to lose matches. Supernatural powers were called upon to win the battles. Did they work? We can never know but many seemed to believe in them. Football, it is a crazy game!

Football rivalries are a part of the game, there are many teams that have disappeared from our football world and with them the rivalries and derbies disappeared. Thank God we still have Dynamos against Highlanders and Caps United versus Dynamos. The quality might be going down, but the rivalries still create excitement among fans, long may that continue.

Chapter 10
Death in the football family: A tribute to the departed Legends!

I remember when we used to sing, "*Good friends we had, good friends we lost along the way... in this great future, you cannot forget the past, so dry your tears!*" Bob Marley comforted us. In Zimbabwe we have a statement, "Pasi hapaguti," literally translated "the earth does not get satiated." We also say "Pasi Panodya. The earth swallows or eats!"

These are both statements which accept the inevitability of death. They seek consolation in the knowledge that as long as we live, death will always be our partner which lingers on the horizon, waiting to pounce. In this journey of life, which is also a journey into football fandom,many friends have died. Friends I played, discussed and watched football with. And yes, many heroes of the game have passed on at the national level. Their deaths left a gaping hole in the football fraternity, more so because most of them died in their prime. Death indeed comes to all in the end but that does not make it any less painful. I dedicate this chapter to the good friends and heroes we lost.

I had many friends. We had many things in common but the one thing which united us the most was football. We played football, we talked football, we fell out over football, but we always found a way to reconcile over football. Football united us and the bond between us was unbreakable.

One of my best friends was Raphael Mukundadzviti known in the neighbourhood as Radza. He loved Dynamos and he prided himself as being a Mbare born and bred "Bornrukisheni", "born and raised in the ghetto" as he called himself. He was proud of his Mbare roots and Dynamos being a club founded in Mbare, it followed that the club was in his blood.Disagreements were therefore inevitable with me in the Caps United corner and my other friend Lawrence Nyatsine, we called him Lule in the Black Rhinos corner. On most weekends, we had some fallouts with Radza boasting about the football prowess of Dynamos while we lauded the strengths of our football teams. The arguments were tense but at the end of it all we kissed and hugged, friends again. Football divided us but brought us together too. Radza was also a good midfielder. He played for fun but could have reached the very top if he had taken the game more seriously. He played many matches at grassroots level and he scored many goals.

Then around the year 2003 he got sick. He was sick for a very long time. By that time, he had moved to Bulawayo and working for the National Railways of Zimbabwe. We still talked about football, argued, but his energy was gone. After close to a year on the sick bed, he succumbed. I mourned for him, gone too soon at the age of thirty-five.

What a loss!

There are others too, like Jimmy, he played football for fun. I called him the juggling expert; he never passed the ball without first trying a trick, a flick or an audacious skill. For him football was entertainment, win or lose, it did not really matter, if he had his bit of fun. This frustrated team mates at times, "Pass the ball Jimmy, Pass the ball!" they berated him. But did Jimmy listen? No! Jimmy was busy doing what he knew best, having fun. It was all fun, the football bond kept us together despite the occasional fallouts.

Again, Jimmy fell sick and after a long illness he died. At his funeral we reminisced about his ball juggling skills. We wondered how far he could have gone with his football if he had committed himself more to the basics of the game rather than just indulge himself all the time.

There was Benjamin Kusena, he called himself "MuJerimani" because he had spend some time studying in East Germany during the communist era. When the Berlin wall fell in 1989 as the hunger for change became irresistible, Kusena came back home without finishing his degree. He was not happy and resorted to drinking to console himself. And when he drank, he talked football, he loved Dynamos and Edward Katsvere. We had discussions which went on well into the night. The more he drank, the wilder his football assertions became but we tolerated that because we knew that deep down something else was eating at his heart. Then he became sick and after a long battle, he succumbed. It was sad, but I will always remember those football discussions.

Alex Nyanga another Dynamos die hard was the same, he drank, argued about football, drank some more and argued again. He too fell ill and after a long struggle, he passed on. These were good friends who left in their prime and I miss them dearly, they were real football friends.

On a National level, death has visited the football fraternity with worrying regularity. Some died in tragic circumstances like accidents while others died after long illnesses. The tragic accidents were especially heartbreaking.

"Breaking news reaching us is that three Caps United players have lost their lives in an accident. They were on their way from a league match in Bulawayo. We will keep you updated as we gather more information!" announced Charles Mabika in an early morning news broadcast on 14 March 2004. The suspense was unbearable as we all started speculating about the identity of the victims. "Have you heard, three Caps United players have died in an accident?" we asked each other. We could not talk about

131

anything else, we could not even work. We waited and waited until Charles Mabika came back with the update. "Blessings 'Yogo Yogo' Makunike, Shingirayi Twaliki and Gary Mashoko are the three Caps United players who lost their lives in a car accident. They were travelling together with two supporters Gibson Murinye and Onesmo Harinye when their vehicle crashed and caught fire" confirmed the veteran journalist.

I felt numb, I could not cry, pictures of the accident kept playing in my head. What made it ghastlier, was the fact that the vehicle had burst into flames and the players were trapped inside! They were literally burnt alive.

It was a tragic, their teammates just watched helplessly, the screams piercing through as life ebbed away from the trapped victims. I was traumatised, and I could not sleep for days. I wonder how the players who saw this hellish scene managed to cope. Cephas Chimedza one of the players said, "I am surprised that I recovered from this horror scene, football lost meaning for me, I just wanted to shut myself in and cry all the time".

The Football administrators gave the team a time to mourn, and the players managed to recover. They galvanised themselves and managed to win the league for their dead comrades.

As a member of the Caps United family, I attended the funeral of these fallen soldiers. The whole Zimbabwe football fraternity was united in grief. I loved Blessing Makunike. What a talent he was! His skills were calling out for a higher league but unfortunately, cruel fate intervened. Shingi Arlon was a reliable goal poacher who could unlock the meanest of defences. Gary Mashoko was an up and coming defender who had his whole career ahead of him. How unfortunate and sad! These were young men who still had so much to offer, indeed, as we say "the earth does not get satiated"; it swallows the young and the old alike.

There was also Watson Muhoni a young and upcoming defender who was so good that the Dynamos faithful had already nicknamed him "Kabila" after the DRC leader who toppled long term dictator Mobuto Seseko. For his bravery and uncompromising defending, the fans decided that Kabila was a suitable name for young Watson Muhoni. The circumstances of his death in 1998 made it even more painful. A hastily arranged challenge match saw a group of Dynamos players embark on a journey to Chivhu which culminated in his fateful road accident death. They were on the off-season, so they decided to play the game to keep their fitness and to make a bit of money on the side. Watson was not keen to go but had second thoughts after talking to then captain, Memory "Mwendamberi" Mucherahowa.

"I am still haunted by the death of Wattie. He did not want to go for the trip. I talked him into changing his mind, little did I know that I was inviting him to his death." said the captain in his recently published biography, *Soul of Seven Million Dreams*. Death comes like a thief, it comes when we least expect it.

On the way, the car carrying the players burst its front wheel and overturned. All the other players were thrown out of the truck and guess who got trapped under the truck? Watson Muhoni was the unfortunate victim. He had tried to dodge the arrow of death by refusing to go on this trip but as fate would have it, he agreed and paid with his life.

No wonder why Memory is still haunted, he had to break the news to Muhoni's family. Where do you start? He still feels culpable and maybe he is understandable that he feels this way. This was a big loss to the Zimbabwe football fraternity, a loss to club and country for indeed Muhoni was a rising star.

Titus Majola was nicknamed "Yellowman" for his very light complexion. He was a midfield workhouse for

Bulawayo giants Highlanders. Then one day in 1988, I returned home to be greeted by my brother's wife, "Babamudiki, have you heard, a Highlanders player has been stabbed to death" she shouted. She could not remember the name for she was not much of football fan.

I had not heard so I waited for the next news bulletin. Those days we did not have phones, there was no social media, the only source of news was the radio, or one had to wait for the morning papers. After an hour the confirmation came, Titus Majola snatched from our midst at the tender age of twenty-nine. The sad part was that he was trying to stop a fight among drinking mates, one of them lost control and plunged a okapi knife into the chest of the peace making Majola. What a senseless loss. The football fraternity mourned Majola and renowned singer Lovemore Majaivana dedicated a song to the fallen midfield maestro. Majola was popular across the football divide, he played with a smile on his face and he gave it all on the pitch. He was committed to the game.

Stanley Ndunduma was a true legend of the Zimbabwe game. Twice in 1981 and 1985, he clinched the ultimate prize in Zimbabwe football, the Soccer Star of the year award. He won numerous trophies with both Caps United and Black Rhinos. He earned numerous caps for the National team and is regarded by many as among the top five players to emerge from the country. Then he decided to go to Swaziland to try his hand at coaching. We all wished him well with his new club aptly named 11 Men in Flight. But death was waiting, one day in 1994, he decided to drive into town for a drink.

The roads in Swaziland are not the safest. How the accident happened, no one has ever sufficiently explained, the news filtered through "Stanley Ndunduma is no more!" What a blow! It took me months to recover from tragic news. Sinyo as we called him was gone, he left us with just the memories.

Oliver Kateya the popular Dynamos and National team left back was also snatched from our midst by a car accident. He was in the company of another former Arcadia United player. Oliver Kateya was a larger than life character of the football fraternity, jovial, full of energy and popular across the football divide. Then one night he went out for a drink with a group of friends. Returning home in the wee hours, he was hit by a car and died on the spot! Tragic, "The Monitoring Force" also known as "The Flying Saucer", gone too soon. The same tragedy befell lethal finisher Adam Ndlovu, another hastily organised friendly match in Kariba between Highlanders legends and a Kariba Select on 16 December 2012 turned tragic. On the way, the car overturned and Adam who was travelling together with his young brother Peter died on the spot. What a loss because Adam was now an upcoming coach and a lot was expected of him. These deaths united the fans, club rivalries were set aside as we mourned the departed heroes.

However, others died after being ill for a while. The trend was familiar, a legend would disappear from the public domain, fans would whisper about his ill health and after a while, the death was announced in the media. It was a difficult time for many fans, many wondered what was eating our legends.

I always wonder what could have happened if these legends had lived long enough to embark on coaching careers. Some had already started on a promising note like the man who made me love football Joel Shambo. Shambo was the man who converted me into a football disciple. He preached the football gospel with his feet, chest, flicks, turns and his handsome physical stature. He also had an illuminating smile. To watch Shambo moving gracefully on the pitch was to watch the beauty of football in all its fullness. He made me create a word "Shamboist ", that is

135

what I call myself. It is a tribute to a man who personified good football for me.

As a coach, Shambo took the flamboyant Blackpool Football Club to the semi final of the African Cup Winners Cup in 1996. With the team he also won the Castle Cup in 1995 and was robbed of the League Championship by a boardroom decision which allowed Dynamos to play their last match on a different day. Dynamos knew what they had to do and scored enough goals to pip Blackpool on goal difference. The injustice was felt by many. These achievements clearly showed what a good coach he was. But death came on 1 May 2000 and claimed him, he was barely forty, what a loss. His death hit me to the core, I mourned him for months.

I have already stated how I fell in love with Zimbabwe football and embarked on this fandom journey. Caps United are the team that made the courtship and I duly accepted. Several players and coaches from that original team that I watched in 1981 have since passed on. These were heroes in our eyes and we considered them as friends close to our hearts. Coaches Obediah "Wasu" Sarupinda, he was a jolly good old fellow and Ashton. "Papa" Nyazika are no more. Tobias Moyo, Joel Shambo, Stanley Ndunduma, Friday Phiri, Oliver Chidemo, Shacky Tauro and Clever Muzuva, I watched them train, I watched them play, they are all gone leaving us with only the memories.

In the Dynamos camp of the 80's I admired many players and some of them are no more. Dribbling wizard Edward "Twinkletoes" Katsvere is one of them, he is no more. There was also one of the best attacking right backs to emerge from the country, Garnett Muchongwe, he is no more. Muchongwe was the type of player who made fans from rival teams, cheer because of his calculated runs on the flanks and pinpoint crosses. What a player he was. Kenneth Jere, Gift Mpariwa, Kuda Muchemeyi, Hamid

Dhana, Lucky Dube, Leo Ntawantawa and David Muchineripi are some of the Dynamos greats of the 80's who have since passed on. Yes, they were football rivals but in the football family we were one, so their death pained us too. The grief is deeply felt.

Highlanders Football Club have lost many stars too the likes of Willard Khumalo, Mercedes Sibanda, Nhamo Shambira, Benjamin Nkonjera, Fanuel Ncube, Tymon Mabaleka, Cleopas Dlodlo, Fanwell Ncube, Nhamo Shambira, Titus Majola, Dumisani Ngulube nicknamed "Chimbi Chimbi," I loved this legend, Ronnie Jowa, Tutani "Toots" Moyo, the list is long. They gave us unforgettable moments and will always be cherished.

The list of legends who have since passed on is long. I hope in future our football authorities will compile a data base of these. Players like David Mwanza, Newman Bizeki, Tobias Moyo, Abraham Mwanza, Alan Jalasi, Tobias Sibanda, Gift Mudangwe, Ashton Mhlanga, Richard Manda, Frank Mukanga are among those who have passed on and are sorely missed. They were good football friends, heroes, we belonged together to the big football family.

Lest I forget, the coaches too like Reinard Fabisch, Stanley Marunza, Peter Nyama, Lovemore Nyabeza, Peter Nyama, Barry Daka, Charles Mandizvidza, Geshom Ntini among others all departed when they still had so much to offer.

Junior coaches like Never Gombera, Jimmy Malomo and Alois Patsika who produced so many great players who graced our fields are also gone. They are often unsung heroes. Club owners like Eric Rosen of Motor Action, Blackpool's Joe Salifu, Joe Masunda, Gorden Chademunhu and others, they contributed to the development of the game and departed. Administrators like the greats Nelson Chirwa and Morrison Sifelani have died. Great referees like the elders of the profession Felix Sanyika and Martin Gede among others have left us and we will always remember them. Tears can dry but the memories will live with us forever.

I also extend my tribute to those who brought us the action through the back pages. Indeed, through their reports, we were able to appreciate the game better, they made us see the game through their words. They became an integral part of the football family and their deaths left a void, which will always be felt. Allan Hlatswayo, Sam Marisa, Tinaye Garande, Phillip Magwaza, Lovemore Musharavati among others have all departed this earth but the articles they penned will live with us forever.

I will include an article written by Sam Marisa, "Caps Hit Dynamos for Seven!" in this narrative. I will have another one of his hard-hitting headline "AFC Leopards Maul Caps United". These were iconic articles, which will live with us forever.

Yes, English language and literature were my favourite subjects and I credit my 'O' Level teacher Mr. Mombeirere for helping me to attain a good grade. But it was also from reading the back pages of The Herald newspaper that I enhanced my language prowess. Sometimes I surprised my friends with the new words that I threw around to spice my conversations and compositions. I borrowed most of them from the Sports Pages.

I became familiar with words such as "saga" when I read about "The Chimutanda Saga." This was after the mercurial midfield genius refused to play for the National Team. He was not happy because Zifa had made no effort to ensure the players against injuries. I became familiar with football metaphors too like that instance when The Herald back page screamed, "Tauro, Shambo Axed!" I was in a shock "Axed!" I thought the two legends had been ambushed by the then notorious Axe Killer who was terrorising residents in Harare around 1984. Lo and behold, after going through the report, I realised that "Axed" simply meant that the two stars had been dropped from the national team. I appreciated football metaphors and understood their use in reports.

"Gweru United buried BAT Ramblers in an avalanche of goals," was another report after the former had put seven past the helpless tobacco makers.Then there was, "Another one bites the dust!" This was when Dynamos fired three past Nigerian giants Shooting Stars in an Africa Champions League tie in 1982. I also became familiar with terms such as "Defence splitting passes", "Versatile", "Dribbling wizard," "Utility player", "maestro" and "Evergreen" to mention just a few. For these and many others, phrases and expressions that I gleaned from the back page, I can only say long live to the memory of these departed wordsmiths. How else could I have known about a "Hat trick" without reading their football reports? They are a football family and sorely missed.

To talk about Zimbabwe football without talking about the football commentators who gave us the action through the radio and later Television will be to leave a yawning gap in our the football narrative. Football commentary reached dizzy heights in the 80's. Many people did not have radios and it was not uncommon for people to go to the shopping centre to just listen to football commentary.

Many commentators came to the fore like Charles Mabika, Evans Mambara, Choga Tichatonga, Lisben Nasasara to name but a few. Out of these mentioned, only Charles "CNN" Mabika is still alive and going strong in his chosen field. He has since been joined by other young commentators but if the truth be said none of them can match those legends of old.

One such great commentator was Evans Mambara, the one with the booming voice, "Black Rhinos, the soldiers are firing from all angles, bomb for bomb, fighting fire for fire."The legendary football commentator would announce himself every Saturday or Sunday afternoon at three

139

oclock! Mambara had this uncanny ability to bring the action on the pitch right into the nation's living rooms. He did it with an energy and enthusiasm that was infectious to all who listened. Listening to Evans on the radio became a Sunday ritual for all of us. He is sorely missed. He died in his prime leaving a gaping hole in the commentary world. Lisben Nasasara and Jonathan Mutsinze were also great commentators in the vernacular languages both Ndebele and Shona, they are sorely missed.

Still in the area of the of vernacular language, Mukoma Choga Tichatonga Gavhure often joined them. When Mukoma Choga Tichatonga Gavhure announced, "Zvinhu zvakaita manyama amire nerongo... the situation is not looking good here," the listeners knew they were not only embarking on a football journey but on a Shona language lesson journey as well. For Mukoma Choga, football commentary provided him with an opportunity to deploy Shona idioms and proverbs as he took the listener on a rich language and football journey. This made his commentaries such a pleasure to listen to. He has since departed this earth but all in the football family will forever cherish his football contributions. These commentators made football listening a hobby for many of us, without them the action would have passed us by because not all fans could go to the stadiums. Listening on radio meant that we could live the action from as a far way places as Muazarabani, Kariba, Murambinda or Beitbridge.

As Evans Mambara used to announce without fail, "Where ever you are, from Zambezi to Limpopo, you might be in Beitbridge, Mutoko, Muzarabani or in Victoria Falls, Dynamos are launching another attack at Highlanders, they have deployed everyone on the battlefront." Or Mukoma Choga saying, "Tirimuno munhandare yeRufaro, vanhu mavhu nemarara, zuva rakacheka nyika, mutambo pakati peDynamos The Glamour Boys ne Highlanders Bosso vave pedyo kutanga,"

140

literally translated to "We are here at Rufaro Stadium, the sun is shining as we await the match to commence." We lived the action through their voices. They were our eyes and these memories are cherished.

Indeed "Pasi Panodya, Pasi hapaguti, the earth devours, it never gets satiated." Our elders left us with this philosophically loaded statement, but even as the football journey continues, I must value the memories of these departed friends and heroes. As a football family, we remember the departed, those who now rest in the cold earth, who cannot read this book. I cannot mention them all, but they are all cherished. All I can say is, "Rest in Peace legends of the game. You will always be remembered!"

Chapter 11
Of teenage prodigies, super subs and foreign stars

We have been blessed with teenage prodigies who have taken our football world by storm leaving us awestruck at their audacious skills. Nothing excites more than a young star who announces himself with a bang especially on the big stage. That young prodigy who sets the match alight is always makes for a good story both for the fans and the press.

Fans also look forward to that special player who can change the momentum of a game from the bench. When a game is not going according to plan, the player with the magical touch can rise from the bench to clinch a winner. With such players, fans fall in love and often demand their introduction and coaches usually oblige by unleashing the game changer from the bench.

Zimbabwe football has also been graced by international stars who have taken our league by storm. It will be amiss not to talk about these stars who came, saw, conquered and departed from our arena leaving us with living memories of their skills. Allow me therefore to share my memories of the prodigies, the super substitutes and the foreign stars who left a permanent imprint on my mind.

"Alois Bunjira is making them jump like Kriss Kross, here he comes again with the ball glued at his feet!" announced veteran football commentator Charles Mabika, the man who used to bring us all the action to our sitting rooms with his booming voice. To listen to Charles Mabika or CNN as we called him was to visualise all the action through his narration. He had that ability to paint the action with his football diction. In this case he also earned Alois Bunjira the baby faced Darryn Textiles striker a new nickname," Kriss Kross." He was deploying his musical knowledge by borrowing the song Jump by this young rap duo Kriss Kross.

Indeed, on this day in 1992 during a replayed Castle Cup match at Rufaro Stadium, Alois Bunjira then a seventeen-year old student at Prince Edward school had announced himself with a bang on the Zimbabwe football stage. Many fans had not heard about Alois and certainly, the Caps United defenders did not expect such a devastating performance from the teenage prodigy.

Maybe it was complacency, maybe they were just off form but whatever it was, Caps United paid a heavy price for underestimating the rookie striker. He gave them a torrid time, made them jump as Charles Mabika kept telling us and capped it all with two goals, his contribution to a four-nil drubbing of the favourites. Fans from both sides of the football divide left the stadium having witnessed something special. Indeed, he turned out to be a special talent who mesmerised defenders with his skills and banged in goals at will. He had a long fruitful career which took him to South Africa but it all started with that big performance during the Castle Cup final at Rufaro stadium.

That Castle Cup final also provided an opportunity for two other teenage prodigies to shine, Alois's best friend and school mate Stewart "Shutto power" Murisa and another virtual unknown to most fans, Felix "Kunyado" Antonio. Stewart was also a student at Prince Edward School and he announced himself on the big stage with a sterling performance on this day. The Alois Bunjira-Stewart Murisa combination was in its early stages, but fans took notice, "Ndevapi vapfanha ava...who are these kids?" the fans kept asking. Well, they were soon to know, the boys went on to be men and conquered the Zimbabwe league with Blackpool and Caps United. At

Caps United, they delivered a first league championship after independence for the Green machine, providing both attacking flair and goals.

What a career they had, they formed a good friendship on and off the pitch, it proved to be one of the best attacking combinations to emerge in our league and that bright Sunday afternoon provided fans with a glimpse of what was to come. The other schoolboy in that team was Felix Antonio, nicknamed Kunyado who was the son of one of the most lethal strikers of the 1970's Chita "Black Mamba" Antonio. The old man had bequeathed his striking prowess to his first-born son and on this day, Felix ran the Caps United defence torrid and capped it all with one goal. Felix completed an attacking trio of three schoolboys on this beautiful Sunday afternoon.

Allan Hansen the deadpan former Liverpool stalwart turned broadcaster later claimed that "You cannot win anything with kids!" when he was dismissing Manchester United's title credentials for the 1995-1996 English Premiership season. The kids who included David Beckham, Gary Neville, Nick Butt, Ryan Giggs and Paul Scholes among others made him eat humble pie by winning the double. If only he had watched this Darryn T team, it would have saved him the embarrassment. For in 1992, four years before his infamous statement, Darryn T had done just that with three schoolboys and a bunch of other talented youngsters like Norman Mapeza and Lloyd Chitembwe who had just finished school but, were still teenagers.

The coach Polish mentor Wieslow Graboswiki had trusted the youth and the youth had delivered a trophy for him. What an achievement this one, all genuine football fans enjoyed it.

Indeed, a number of schoolboys were so good that most Super league teams in the 80's had no hesitation to throw them into the deep end. They were rewarded with

144

match winning performances. At my school, St. Peter Kubatana we had Francis Nechironga and Christopher Chavhungama. While still in Form Four, Francis Nechironga broke into the star-studded Caps United team of the 80's.

It was a team full of stars, the young men often described as "bustling striker" was able to hold his own. When he went to Lesotho for a continental assignment with the team, the whole school was proud of him. Our bespectacled Headmaster, Mr Dupwa made a special announcement at assembly about the new hero. We shared the glory as students for one of our own was rubbing shoulders with football royalty.

Christopher Chavhungama, I have already narrated his story, was another teenage prodigy among us who was mixing up with the stars of the game while playing for BAT Ramblers. At about the same time, Dynamos the biggest club in the country were brave enough to play George Munjanja who was a student at George Stark Secondary school. He even scored in a midweek game under flood lights. To have his name in the sports section of the country's largest daily newspaper The Herald was a remarkable achievement for the schoolboy.

On that day, he played with another teenage sensation Alois Bikwa who was a student at Rusununguko College. These were the days when schools football was highly competitive, many young players emerged to play for the established teams. Indeed, schools can be an incubator of talent and continue to do so if school leaders allow enough time for students to play sport.

The second term used to be reserved for football, students loved this term. New heroes emerged, and we were spoiled for entertainment. Now the school leaders have decided to stage galas, crunching all the matches in one weekend with teams playing only twenty minutes. This has stunted the growth of school football and I urge them to rethink this approach.

Sometime in 1987 during a night game, Dynamos played perennial rivals Caps United at Rufaro Stadium. On this night, a new star was born, and he left then Herald Sports Editor Jahoor Omar waxing lyrical. He wrote, "The name Gift Mudangwe might not be a household name in the Zimbabwe football fraternity but ask any fan who watched the match last night, they will now admit that they know him!" Gift Mudangwe, the Marist High schoolboy had delivered a devastating performance which left seasoned defender Garnett Muchongwe wishing that he had faked injury to avoid facing the young star. Mudangwe had pace to burn, he had dribbling skills galore and, on this night, he unleashed both qualities on the unsuspecting Dynamos defence with devastating effect. By the end of the night Caps United had triumphed by three goals to win but the night belonged to Mudangwe the schoolboy prodigy. What a player he went on to be.

I also remember a young star Dumisani Ngulube of Highlanders who as a sixteen-year-old school boy, came to Rufaro with Highlanders and scored an overhead kick to knock Dynamos out of the Rothmans Cup. He became an immediate hero to the black and white army of Highlanders fans. He went on to make some telling contributions for the team although his career was short lived. Willard Khumalo also established himself in a star-studded Highlanders team while still a school boy at Northlea high school. So, did Peter Ndlovu who took the Zimbabwe football fraternity by storm, for two years he was unstoppable and it all started when he was a schoolboy at Mzilikazi High school, that hotbed of football talent in the city of Kings, Bulawayo. Of all the schoolboys in the Zimbabwe football narrative, I think Peter had the greatest impact.

There is a time when Dynamos decided to focus more on the junior teams with the aim of grooming stars of the future. To achieve this, they partnered Churchill High school, a school which used to dominate high school football in Zimbabwe. Several Dynamos junior players were enrolled at the school to continue with their education while at the same time turning up for Dynamos.

Many of them played in the reserve side but a few broke through and took the Zimbabwe premier league by storm. Cephas Chimedza was one of them. He was so good that at sixteen years he was a regular feature of the Dynamos first team. He was versatile and could play in a number of positions, left back, defensive and attacking midfielder. He exuded amazing confidence on the pitch for one so young. It did not come as a surprise therefore when in 2004, two years after starting his career, he was crowned as the Soccer star of the year award, an award which confirmed him as one of the legends of the game in the country.

His teammate at Churchill High School and Dynamos was Norman Maroto a lethal finisher, maybe one of the best to emerge from this factory of talent. "Schoolboy Maroto saves Dynamos again!" was not an uncommon headline to read from the sports pages of Zimbabwe's largest daily paper, The Herald. He was a born predator in the box and whenever he was on the pitch fans knew that a goal would come. I remember very well many pictures of him in the papers celebrating another goal. Even for rival fans, this was something beautiful to behold, a young star being born. Other young stars who made an impact while still at the school were Leo Kurauzvione for Dynamos and Clement Mutawu for Motor Action. It was also good to see Clement Mutawau clinching the prestigious Soccer star of the year in 2006. This is another fitting tribute to this great school that contributed to the development of Zimbabwe football.

Indeed, many schools played their role in developing football talent in Zimbabwe and many schoolboys were able to play for big clubs even as they also played for their school teams. Maxwell Dube from Ascot High school in Gweru went on to win the Soccer Star of the year award in 2001 but he broke into the Chapungu team as a mere sixteen-year-old. What a tricky winger with a fierce shot he turned out to be.

Ian Matondo later captained a star studded under twenty-three Zimbabwe Warriors and was tipped as a future senior Warriors captain. Sadly, he lost his way along the football journey, but he had started so well as a schoolboy at Sakubva High school. He commanded a regular place in the Tanganda Football Club team which took Zimbabwe football by storm. Others like goalkeeper Nelson Bandura and Spencer Ngove who were at Mutare Boys High also broke into the team and made it such a formidable outfit.

There are so many teenage schoolboys who made their mark and for this I must thank the schools. They nurtured the talent and I think it is now time to revisit the development trajectory. Schools such as Mzlikazi, Msiteli, Mpopoma, Prince Edward, Churchill, St Peters Kubatana, Sakubva High, Hippo Valley and many others dotted around the country should rediscover that zeal to develop talent. To achieve this more qualified coaches must work in schools to nurture the talent. Retired legends should be capacitated to visit schools in all corners of the country to impart football knowledge. This will serve a double purpose the legends are gainfully employed and the kids benefit from the coaching. It is a win win situation, Zifa and the Sports Commission should seriously consider this.

Schools should also dedicate the second term to ball games and football will be prominent again. Nowadays many schools are staging galas and it is such decisions by

148

school leaders that have cost the sport heavily. I hope they have a rethink of this strategy.

Let me now talk about another aspect of our football which I find fascinating. Dear reader, allow me to pay tribute to the hero from the bench, the weapon to be deployed when the going gets tough. The impact player or the super substitute as we called them from the terraces also generate a lot excitement among football fans.

In my football journey and experience, I have seen many such heroes of our game. In the 1980s when my journey started in full throttle, I witnessed a number of game changers who could come in and change the complexion of the game. One such player was Nhamo Shambira of Highlanders. The diminutive striker always made a difference whenever he came in a substitute. His introduction always generated excitement among the fans because they were assured of a goal.

The moment he stood up from the bench to start his warm up routine, the atmosphere would suddenly change, fans knew that something was about to happen and happen it did. Nhamo always delivered changing the mood of his supporters from gloom to celebration. In the same team there was Tobias Mudyambanje who was another game changer, every time he was introduced. He made an impact often converting half chances to earn victory for his team. Dumisani Ngulube, another striker, was often introduced from the bench. I have already talked about his debut match when he scored with an overhead kick soon after being introduced. He cemented his reputation as a super sub with that goal against Dynamos.

Caps United had the affable Mukoma Oliver Chidemo, everyone called him "Bla Ole ". He often sat on the bench because of Shacky Tauro but when he got his chance to come in, he never disappointed. In the late 80's, Never Chiku came to the fore, fans knew that the introduction of this super sub would claim victory for his club. He became a cult hero especially as he always seemed to do well against perennial rivals Dynamos. He seemed to enjoy scoring against big goalkeeper Peter Fanuel. This endeared him in the hearts of the Green Army as Caps United fans prefer to call themselves.

Later in 1996 as the club was chasing its first league win, a new bulky hero who literally proved to be a handful for the defenders emerged. The fans called him "Yokozuna," a nickname derived from the Japanese wrestlers who threw their weight around in the ring. Simon Dambaza had body mass and he used it to good effect, shielding the ball away from defenders. He also had the pace that defied his bulky physic and an eye for goal. With these attributes, he was often used as a weapon of choice by coach Steven "The Cool Dude" Kwashi who deployed him with one simple instruction, "Go and win the game for us!" Dambaza never let his coach down. He always delivered. What an impact he had as Caps United became Zimbabwe Champions in 1996.

The world over, super subs are well respected with Ole Gunnar Solskjaer of Manchester United the ultimate hero for many. In one match, he was introduced in a match against Nottingham Forest with only eighteen minutes to go. By the end of the match, he had scored four goals. Well no substitute had this same effect in our football league but like stated above, we still had our own heroes from the bench, they deserve some paragraphs in this football narrative.

No Nation is an island. No football leagu lives in splendid isolation. Nations depend on each other, people move and look for work in in various countries. Football players are no exception and Zimbabwe has been fortunate to have foreign stars come to her league. I have often argued that one of the reasons why the English Premier league improved so dramatically was the influx of foreign players and coaches.

The arrival of players like Gianfranco Zola, Dennis Bergkamp, Eric Cantona, Patrick Viera, Nwako Kanu among others made the English realise that there was another way to play football apart from kick and rush. Football can be beautiful and the foreign stars like Zola and Bergkamp showed how this was possible. Well in Zimbabwe, we also benefitted from the influx of internationals especially from our northern neighbours Zambia. It will therefore be amiss to complete this chapter of my football experiences without hailing these foreign heroes.

My first port of call must be Lizwe Chafunya, the Malawian international who had a stint with Highlanders. He was an attacking right back who brought a lot of excitement to the league. This was around 1983 and I think he was the first import to grace the Super League after independence. He later moved to South Africa, but he remains a Highlanders Legend.

One of the best import from Malawi to grace the Zimbabwe league was Joseph Kamwendo who played for Caps United. He was a dynamic midfielder and pulled the strings in the middle of the park as Caps United stormed to another title in 2005. The selectors of the prestigious Soccer Star of the year award were so impressed that they did something that had never been done before, crown him King of Zimbabwe football for that year. He became the first foreigner to clinch the award and his place in the annals of Zimbabwe football history was cast in stone. In that same swashbuckling Caps United line up, there were two other foreign stars from Zambia, Laughter Chilembe and Ian Bakala.

Laughter had a funny football name but that was the only comic thing about him. He was a solid defender who could carry the ball from defence and initiate attacks. He is among the top ten defenders to play for Caps United's long history. Ian Bakala was a winger who could also play as an attacking midfielder. He was a bit of a showman but what a player he was. The three foreign stars made Caps United such a well-oiled machine and the fans will always remember them for their contribution.

Other Zambians who left a huge impression are Charles Chilufya at Hwange FC and Highlanders, Ferdinand Mwachindalo at Amazulu FC and Masvingo United and Kelvin Kaiundu at Highlanders. They were all midfielders and they added value to the teams they played for. Ferdinand was a defensive midfielder who played for Amazulu and Masvingo United.

With Amazulu he won the league championship. He was tireless, he was known for his leadership qualities. For this he was made captain. When he was at Masvingo United he also showed his willingness to work hard and once more he was made captain. Mwachindalo was a born leader. The other midfield workhorse was Charles Chilufya. He was tireless and was made captain of Highlanders which is no mean feat. He played with his heart and I rate him as one of the best midfielders of his generation. Kelvin Kaiundu was renowned for his football acumen a midfield thinker and he became a fan favourite. When his playing career was over, he returned to coach the club further cementing his legendary status among the Highlanders faithful.

Dabitswa Nkoma for Rail Stars, Francis Kasanda, Sandras Kamwenda and Clive Mwale all for Dynamos are the other Zambian internationals who graced our league and made a positive impact. However, allow me to talk about one of the most frustrating players to grace the league. George Owusu who played for Caps United and Dynamos. He was one of the most talented dribblers and good user of the ball I have watched. However, he just did not care, he rarely put an effort and treated football as a pastime. If a pass did not come to his feet, he would just let it go without trying to chase.

When others were hustling and fighting for the ball, George Owusu would be standing, hands on his waist, a virtual spectator. Fans indulged him for a while because when his mood was right he did produce moments of unforgettable genius. But these moments were rare, and, in the end, he will be remembered for lack of effort on the pitch that for his football skills. What a disappointment.

Webster Chikabala another Zambian international was an accomplished midfielder, he was a capable dribbler who played for Darryn Textiles and later became the player coach of Mhangura Football club. He was also great. I however save the best for last. Derby Makinka, what a player!

He joined Darryn T in 1990 and stayed for only eight games but thirty years later we still talk about this midfield genius who took Zimbabwe football by storm. Derby had a unique football name, he had the skills, the football arrogance and the football intelligence to win matches single handedly. For those eight games he mesmerised fans with his audacious skills and cheeky dribbles. Watching Derby Makinka was to watch football poetry in motion, he was the very personification of the beautiful game. Dummies, flicks, inch perfect passes, gazelle like runs across the pitch, the cocky personality and yes, the goals, Derby was indeed a complete package. Despite the short stint, his contribution will always be cherished, and the football pundits included him among the best eleven players in the league for 1990 season. About Derby Makinka I can safely say, "He came, he saw, and he conquered!". He left for Europe and three years later, he was dead.

On 27 April 1993 a dark shadow covered the African football terrain, twenty-five Zambian Internationals and five crew members perished in a helicopter crash of the coast of Gabon. They were on their way to Senegal for a World Cup qualifier. It was a tragic accident which is still difficult to accept some twenty-seven years later. Among the thirty victims, Derby Makinka was there. It was a hard blow to take for all of us who had seen him work his magic on our football fields. He died in the service of his country with other gallant sons of nation of Zambia. What a loss, hard to take, to understand and to accept!

I hope this is a fitting tribute to all the teenage stars, super substitutes and the foreign legends who graced our league. I have not mentioned them all, not out of disrespect, but I hope this sample is a fair representation of these various categories. My rich football journey would not have been complete without dedicating a chapter to these football greats. They made football so much fun and the experiences they gave us in their various capacities will forever be cherished.

Chapter 12
The good and the bad!

In the village that I grew up, football was played. My participation as I intimated in the opening chapter was on the sidelines as a cheerleader to the primary school heroes who slugged it out on the dusty pitches. Football is indeed the people 's game played at all levels, the lowest and the highest. It will be amiss not to pay tribute to all those who made and continue to make my football experience such a pleasure.

The fans, the players, the club owners who poured millions and yes, the social league players who are so committed to the game that despite nursing debilitating hangovers, they are still able to come out for a kick about on a Saturday or Sunday morning. It is not easy, but the players know that the best way to treat a hangover is not by drinking some more but by sweating it on the pitch. Football is indeed an outlet, a cure for many of our self-induced ills. Let me look at the good and the bad of my football experience.

Yes, from Zambezi to Limpopo on many of the dusty pitches littered around the country, football is played. Most of this happens far away from the gaze of the media but that does not make the football less exciting. Kids of all age groups, on the streets, in schools and other informal games spend their time enjoying the game of football. There are legends of the game at this level, heroes who will be asked to commit to a team.

"So-and-so is ours!" kids proclaim, eager to have the star of the neighbourhood in their team. At school the rivalry and competition can be equally intense and exciting but now the narrative is changing.

Everyone who grew up in Zimbabwe in the 80s, 90s and early 2000 will remember the football derbies at school level. I had the pleasure of being involved in one such derby during my working stint in Chipinge. I remember that Mt Selinda High school hated to lose against Gaza High School. The great town versus rural divide fuelled this rivalry. Gaza High School was in the centre of Chipinge Town while Mt. Selinda was thirty-seven kilometres away to the east. It therefore followed that Gaza High Students regarded themselves as street smart and viewed students in at Mt Selinda as country bumpkins. However, Mt. Selinda High School was an A level school while Gaza High School only offered Ordinary level studies.

All these little matters were then incorporated into the football, so the matches took an even bigger significance. Matches were tense, and it was not uncommon for them to be abandoned with the losing school accusing the referee of bias. Something good however came from these encounters, good players were developed who went on to play Premier league football in Zimbabwe. Gaza High produced Eddie Dube and Lovemore Mapuya while Mt, Selinda produced Malvern Matselele and Zebediah Chauke.

There were many such blood and thunder rivalries at this level. Mutare Boys High against Marist Nyanga, Churchill High School versus Prince Edward, Cranborne or Glenview High, Mzilikazi High against Hippo Valley at National level or against Churchill High School. This was high school football at its best and many good players emerged from these competitions. All this has changed now. The joy of just playing should not be taken away, but I have seen this happening at an alarming rate in the motherland. I have already highlighted how schools used to nurture talented players.

This role is fast being eroded by adults who have reduced school football to a one-day event through the introduction of galas in schools. The argument is that this will cut the costs that the schools face in feeding the children at weekends. I fail to understand how this decision was arrived at since students can easily walk to and from matches and can carry packed lunch.

However, the school leaders in their wisdom or lack of it decided to go down that road thereby depriving the school kids the opportunity of playing and watching football every weekend. This I feel takes away the joy of school football, something that I used to enjoy as I was growing up. I hope that there will be a rethink, that someone can reverse this decision so that the kids can rediscover that joy of old.

We also live in a winner take all jungle with any opportunity to make an extra dollar grabbed with relish. It is the dog-eat-dog mentality, a selfish approach which has infiltrated our society. Allow me some latitude so I can reinforce my point with a personal experience I encountered. One day on my way to work, I passed through Zengeza 3 football pitch. It was a popular pitch used by all the teams in the locality, it was also used by the local social league club, the one commonly referred as Boozers.

I will talk more about this league and my team, but first to this encounter that captures the selfishness which has gripped our Nation. As I was passing through, I saw one guy busy shovelling sand into a small wheelbarrow which he had brought along for that purpose. I was baffled, I was taken aback! How could someone disregard the whole community of sports lovers who depended on the pitch to exhibit their skills and decide to dig for sand right in the middle of the pitch. For me, this was an unacceptable desecration, an abomination which offended the football God! I decided to confront him, "My friend, what do you think you are doing?" I asked.

He gave a long explanation about the need to plaster his small grocery shop, the one we all know as "tuckshops".

So, the sand from the pitch was his easiest route to achieve that. The small shop for him was more important that the needs of the whole community. I stood my ground and told him, in no uncertain terms, that he had to put the sand back and fill up the gaping hole he had just created in the middle of the pitch. Since a small crowd was now gathering he felt obliged to do that but not before he uttered a few unprintable words in my direction. He was clearly unhappy to be thwarted of his cherished dream of plastering his shop with sand from the community football pitch! What an abomination!

Unfortunately, this incident is not isolated, it is occurring every day. The cannibalism of football pitches in urban centres has meant that one day we will wake up with no space left for the young people to play. The responsible authorities are keen to create a concrete jungle. Many houses have been built on football pitches depriving everyone of playing places. This disease is rife in the urban areas, but the rural areas have not been spared too. Chiefs are parcelling out pieces of land leaving very little space for anything else. At a higher level, we have seen stadium getting dilapidated under the watch of authorities who are supposed to look after them and bequeath them to future generations. Gwanzura Stadium has not hosted matches for over five years.

This is a stadium which is close to my heart with cherished memories. Rufaro Stadium, the spiritual home of our football is on the brink of closure unless someone takes it upon themselves to fix the playing surface. The pride of the Nation, the National Sports Stadium is no longer the home of our National Team, unloved by its owners the Ministry of local Government and condemned by those who run football, Fifa. Cam and Motor Stadium the home of once mighty and now defunct Rio Tinto is no more, dead and buried amidst the carnage that has become the story of our football. Mhangura, Dzivarasekwa, Chibuku, the uniquely named Baghdad in Kwekwe and yes even small ones like Glen Norah Stadium have all become relics of a bygone era, an era when our football was at its peak.

It was an era which made me fall in love with Zimbabwe football. Now all I can hold to are the memories and nothing else. When did this rain begin to beat us? I keep wondering. How did we allow our stadiums to fall into pieces like this? We are a proud people, we pride ourselves as the most literate, on the African continent, yet we have watched helplessly as our football stadiums have become unplayable. Where is the leadership? The fans, the owners of the game, why have they kept silent? I did stand up for that small pitch in Zengeza 3, but on a National level we have watched helplessly as this cherished football heritage disappears.

We have also lost so many clubs and the fans who supported these clubs. Clubs such as Mhangura, Rio Tinto, Blackpool, Gweru United, Shabanie Mine, Ziscosteel, Lancashire Steel, Bata Power, BAT Ramblers, Tanganda United, Zimbabwe Saints, Arcadia United, Black Aces, Motor Action, Monomotapa, Gunners, Amazulu, Shushine, Eagles, Olympics have sunk into oblivion as the economic hardships continue to bite.

These are clubs which gave us some unforgettable moments, clubs which gave us great players. I watched most of these teams and they still hold a special place in my heart. Most of these teams lost their sponsorship due to the harsh economic climate in our country. Mine teams like Rio Tinto, Ziscosteel, Mhangura and Shabanie were affected by the closure of the mines thereby affecting whole communities and the teams. They produced great players who graced our league like the evergreen Joseph Zulu, Ephert Lungu, Rafael Phiri, Barnabas Likombola, and Robert Godoka of Rio Tinto.

I admired Rio Tinto for their super fit players, they always looked like players from another planet. Ziscosteel gave us the likes of Bernard Zikhali, James Takavada, Ephraim Dzimbiri, Newman Bizeki and top goalkeeper Frank Mkanga. What about Shabanie Mine with the likes of Thomas "Chaurura" Makwasha and Asani Juma, these two formed a deadly partnership. It made the team a force to reckon with.

I remember Black Aces a Highfield based club which gave us the likes of Archford Chimutanda, Fresh Chamarenga, the twins Wilfred and William Mugeyi, deadly strikers Stanley "Jaws" Mashezha and Percy "Master" Mwase and midfield stars like Peter Gogoma and Moses "Gwejegweje" Chasweka. Arcadia United represented the coloured community with pride and gave us one of the deadliest strikers to grace the league, George Rollo. Bata Power with the likes of Samson "Chunky" Phiri, Onias Musana, Rainos Mapfumo, lazarus Pararayi and my favourite Zacharia "Lamola" Chironda. The babyfaced assassin who was Wonder Chaka from Gweru United, was a top marksman. I have sweet memories of these teams but indeed I cannot mention all the players.

The teams that I watched had so many good players and even the so called small teams still played fantastic football. Shushine a Zvishavane based outfit which had the likes of Tavaka Gumbo and Isaac Riyano, top midfielders who made it a competitive outfit. To be honest, there were very few poor matches, most teams produced moments to savour.

I also must appreciate the fans, the twelfth man for any team. Dynamos have their " seven million supporters,"

Caps United have their " Green Army," Bosso the "Black and White" army and Gweru United had their "Pisa Pisa" supporters with their paper burning antics. Blackpool had the " Ndochi" dancers and singers and Arcadia had Auntie Cookie with her "Come on Arcadia!" cry.

As a collective the fans always gave their all but there were some outstanding individuals as well who stood out. I had a cousin, Darlington Sidhindi. He is one man who never missed a Dynamos match at home or away. Back in the 80's he hitchhiked to Zaire for a champion's league game between Dynamos and Lupopo Football club. There were many such committed supporters who gave there all in support of their teams. Fans such as Taribo West, Freddy Mugadza and Chris Romario Musekiwa who would go to extraordinary lengths to support their teams.

Each team in the league had many such die hard supporters and some of them took matters to extreme by engaging in hooliganism. In all the stadiums in the country many matches have been abandoned as fans took matters. This was the ugly face of football that needs to be addressed to make football the beautiful game it is supposed to be.

The good and the ugly, it is all part of our football. I pay tribute to the good, like those businessmen who poured millions of dollars into football by supporting their teams. Many of them did it for the love of the game. They did not get any monetary rewards except the satisfaction of promoting the game of football. My football narrative cannot be complete without giving these heroes their place in the history of our game. Lovemore Gijima Msindo of Fire Batteries, Ronnie Chihota, Ginger Chinguwa, Ben Muchedzi, Joe Pajero Masenda, Joel Salif, Chris Sambo and Lecturer Mpala flamboyant businessmen who gave us flamboyant Blackpool Football Club, Delma Lupepe of Amazulu, Twine Phiri who saved Caps United from extinction, Tanda Tavaruva of Masvingo United, John

Nyamasoka with Rufaro Rovers and Hall of Shushine Football club. Even behind the scenes there are many who have never directly owned clubs but are recognised as benefactors of the clubs.

Big Clubs like Highlanders and Dynamos have always benefitted from passionate business people who have poured millions into the clubs. I remember one business person from Highfield, we called him Mudhara Manjoro. He owned a restaurant and every match day he hosted the Black Aces players. Mounds and mounds of sadza and meat were eaten at this restaurant at Machipisa Shopping Centre; this was his way of giving back to the team he loved. Many such committed people have helped various clubs.

However, there were bad incidences as well like the unfair contracts that were given to young players. Excited to be signing their first contract, they did so without reading between the lines. Football owners such as Francis Zimunya, Lovemore Gijima Msindo and even Polish mentor Weislaw Grabowski have been accused of tying down players to contracts if ten years. Critics have described this as a form of slavery and exploitation. Some of the cases that I have come across seem to sustain this criticism. The issue of age cheating has also come to the fore with many club owners accused of doctoring documents so that their players remain marketable on the international arena.

An unsavoury incident also happened when former President of Zimbabwe Canaan Banana who used to own State House Tornadoes was accused of sexually molesting his players. Although only one player openly came to read the charge sheet, rumour has it that this abuse was a daily occurrence. For a man long regarded as Zimbabwe's number one football fan accusations of homosexuality came as a rude shock among culturally conservative Zimbabweans. This was a National scandal which reverberated long in football circles. It left a black mark on our football narrative. Questions are still being asked, hushed discussions but the full list of the abused players has never been fully revealed.

There are many good stories to tell about the football terrain. Take for instance the football families, how many have we had. From the days of the Chieza brothers to the Ndlovu brothers, our football narrative has been replete with families that have graced our league. The Chiezas had George, Winston, Tendai, Itai, Isaac Hector, Patrick and Ian who at one stage all played for Mhangura Football Club. That was an amazing story, a unique one for the country.

While this was in the 1970s, after independence we had many such brothers who graced our league. The Ndlovu brothers became the most prominent due to the exploits of Peter Ndlovu who later played for Coventry City in England. He was the youngest of three brothers who all represented Zimbabwe National team and set the league ablaze with their talent. Adam and Madinda were both great players. We also had Sunday and Misheck Marimo, top defenders for Dynamos and Zimbabwe who later coached the Zimbabwe National team.

The Chieza story of seven brothers in the team was almost replicated by the Matondo brothers of Tanganda who had Revai, Cliff, Ian and Rutherford all doing duty for the Mutare outfit. That is four brothers in the same team another interesting statistic. The Nechironga brothers were two Francis and George, so were the Dhana brothers, Majid and Hamid.

The Chungas came as three, Moses the star of the show, his elder brother Kembo and younger sibling Dixon. The list is long, Emmanuel and Givemore Nyahuma, Stanley and Ernest Chirambadare, John, Davies and Farai Mbidzo. The Mbidzo family gave us one of the best passers of the ball to grace our league, Farai. He was so good the

163

fans gave him the moniker" Mr. Perfect." He was simply unbelievable.

This is just a glimpse into the world of Zimbabwe football families and not an exhaustive list.

There are so many interesting facets about the Zimbabwe football league some of which can be recorded in the Guiness book of records. For example, between 2010 and 2013, goal difference had to be used to decide the champions. This is a riveting piece of history, when Dynamos Football club won three consecutive titles beating their rivals by goal difference. Has this ever happened before in the world? I do not think so and our football scribes led by veteran writer Robson Sharuko have made a case for this to be included in the world book of records. "PAKAANGU", they have decided to call this unique phenenomena. This is a play on the first two letters of the coaches involved in this drama, Pasuwa of Dynamos, Kaindu of Highlanders, Antipas of Chicken Inn and Gumbo of FC Platinum. These coaches and their teams wrote an engrossing piece of history never seen before and I hope this story will be recognised at a world level. I say good luck to Sharuko and his team in this endeavour for indeed it is a good story to tell about our football.

Another interesting facet of our football are the names of players who have graced our league. I think if a competition is to be held on the most unique names in world football Zimbabwe will give many nations a run for their money. From Sunday Marimo, Sunday Masauso, Friday Phiri, July Sharara to Salad Twaliki, Ocean Mushure, Heavens Chinyama, Knowledge Musona, Marvellous Nakamba, the sweet-sounding Melody Wafawanaka to the tough sounding Hardlife Zvirekwi, the fresh sounding Fresh Chamarenga, Mackereza Navaya and Musareka Janitala, Zimbabwe football have given us all sorts of names. However, the reason why I think our league can win any names competition is for only one name, Have A

Look Dube. Allow me to declare this as the most unique name ever given to a player the world over. Have A Look, what a name, the parents deserve a prize for being so creative!

I can also to the names of the clubs such as Lengthens, Kiglon, Tripple B, Buymore, Suri Suri, Hard Body, Boronia Farm and Unique Select, then a world cup of names will surely be won by Zimbabwe. There are many such names but let me just use these as a glimpse once more into our own unique football world which makes it so interesting.

What about the endless and often tense football debates, this is what makes football such an engaging sport. The heated discussions at the various stadiums and even when match is over they are continued in the various pubs. With the advent of social media, these can become acrimonious.

Forget about the Messi versus Ronaldo never ending debate, in Zimbabwe we are equally engaged with who is the greatest? Is it Moses Chunga, George Shaya or Peter Ndlovu? It is fair to say, this can be a tense discussion that can see the best of mates falling out. My take? I will go with George Shaya, the Mastermind! Numbers do not lie. What he achieved in ten or so years at the top, winning the Soccer Star of the year award a record five times puts him in a class of his own.

One friend, Lawrence Nyatsine, the one I call Nyati is always quick to retort, "Yes the Mastermind won it five times, but have you ever wondered what would have happened if Peter had stayed another five years in our league. He had already won it twice. Maybe he could have won it another five years putting good old Shaya in the shade." He argues always.

Against this hypothetical scenario, I must concur, this was indeed a possibility. This debate is difficult to end, Mose Chunga the Razorman might have found a perfect answer to this age-old discussion in his own imitable way,

"George Shaya was the best of his generation, I was the best of my generation and Peter Ndlovu was the best of his generation!" he declared. What a way to resolve a difficult debate.

We have debates about who was the best midfielder, was it Shambo, Mtizwa, Chimutanda, David Mwanza, Bonface Makuruzo, Willard Khumalo, the list is endless? Who was the greatest passer of the ball? Chimutanda, Mtizwa, Shambo, Gidiza Sibanda, Isaac Riyano, Lloyd Mutasa or Farai Mbidzo? It is difficult to agree. What about the best defender, the best goalkeeper? Dear reader, this is what makes football such an engaging game. Everyone has an opinion and every opinion is valid. Only those who lack discursive skills are a danger to this exciting football culture. So many stories to tell. What about the veterans like Chipo Tsodzo, Brighton Chandisaita, Menard Mupera, Mkokheli Dube, Clement Mutawu, players who as individuals clocked two years on the playing pitches of Zimbabwe. Ashton " Musharukwa" Mhlanga, a veteran left back who always dispatched the penalties awarded to Gweru United with aplomb. Legend has it that he never missed one in his twenty years of taking them. Wow! One can only marvel.

We have also had the Castle Soccer Star award that commenced in 1969. It is still a part of the football culture up to this day. The sponsors, Natbrew have been loyal and all-weather friends and they deserve to be celebrated for showing such a commitment to our football journey. Many stars have been rewarded for their performances and many have deserved it.

However, there has been an ugly side as the politics of the media profession often took centre stage in the voting process. Zimbabwe sports journalists often canvassed for players from their respective regions to win the award. Often because the journalists had favourite players from their teams, professionalism was often thrown out of the window resulting in the wrong players being selected. For example, if there was a danger of their favourite losing, votes were then canvassed for a lesser deserving player to win and the real winner would lose out.

In 1989, Stanford "Stix" Mtizwa had a brilliant season even by his own high standards. Everyone expected Stixe as we called him to clinch the coveted award that year. Stix himself was convinced that it was going to be his year! From the blue, the selectors pulled out the proverbial rabbit from the hat as they crowned Masimba Dinyero of Black Mambas. Masimba was good, he was tireless but the battle to save his team from relegation was futile, the team was demoted and now Masimba was getting on the podium to receive the most cherished individual football award in the country.

This was a travesty of football justice. It was daylight robbery and without casting aspersions on the football talents of Masimba Dinyero, it is justified to say the selectors were anti football when they made this selection. The case of Walter Chuma in 1997 also followed similar fault lines as he won it ahead of favourites Englebert Dinha and Tauya Murehwa, this was another miscarriage of football justice. Vitalis Takawira can also feel aggrieved for missing out on the award. Apparently, he drove his manager's car without permission and for that the selectors punished him for lack of discipline.

What about the case of Joseph Zulu – the Rio Tinto slippery winger? He was among the finalist for ten seasons, but not once did he clinch the award. He was indeed the true definition of the perennial football bridemaid. To date, no one can give a satisfactory explanation to this glaring anomaly.

The award remains the most cherished in our football fraternity, but the selection process has not often been carried out with the integrity it deserves thereby bringing out the ugly side of our football.

In football, the focus is often at the high table, the higher leagues but it will be amiss not to mention the social leagues where most of the aspiring players spend most of their time. Even those over the hill, the ones on their last legs come to this league to squeeze out a few old tricks from their tired legs. In most cases, the alignment between what will in the head and what the legs can still do is not always there, but the effort cannot be faulted. It is a league where those who could not quite make it, those trying to make it and those whose best days are over often meet. This league, which started as a Boozers' League, has become decent enough to attract a few very good players. I enjoyed playing in this league very much.

I was part of many teams but the one which stands out for me was Towerlight Rovers. This was a unique name arrived at because the team used to gather under the tower light at Zengeza 3 Shopping centre. This was the meeting point before matches and for the post match ritual of rib tickling tales and the mandatory waters of wisdom in all their forms. It was fun, I interacted with interesting characters like Chipembere, Fatso and Jerry, characters who still make me smile every time I think about them.

What a time that was, a rich deposit in the bank of memory! I think many share these experiences where ever they have played in this league. It is a special league where the game can be enjoyed without pressure. It is a league which is about enjoying and forming comradeships. Now you understand dear reader why I fought so hard to preserve that small football pitch which the small minded aspiring businessman sought to destroy by digging for sand right at the centre of the pitch. I repeat, it was an abomination!

Unfortunately, that pitch which I tried to defend is now surrounded by houses which are slowly threatening to swallow it. I hope the powers that be can preserve what remains of the pitch so that teams like Towelight Rovers and all the young kids in the neighbourhood can have somewhere to play. The social league must be preserved at all cost.

Pardon me for concluding this narration on a sad note, the post playing plight of our legends, the ones who used to attract a multitude of admirers and who made us pack stadiums. They are often reduced to paupers when their careers are over.

I accept that the harsh economic climate has affected all and sundry but when poverty visits our football legends it makes for a sorry sight. I think more needs to be done to empower the players so that they can continue to live dignified lives. It is important to keep former players relevant to the game and can be trained as coaches to work with junior teams. They can also work as coaches in schools and the ministry can facilitate this move.

However, coaching can only absorb a few ex players so business seminars should be held to help empower the legends with business skills so that they can use. There is no shame for the retired legends to embark on new ventures like painting and decorating, building, motor mechanics and farming. I am proud of those legends who have managed to find themselves in a new world without the cheering crowds, it is not always easy. They have to do it because the post playing world can be cruel . Many have found new professions. Others are still involved with football at various levels. My wish is for them to continue in the game, but it might not be possible for all of them. As such, many of them will have to follow completely different routes but what should not happen is to see pauperised former football stars. It is heartbreaking!

Yes the good and the bad often mix in our football fraternity but I must admit I have had more pleasurable experiences that the bad ones. I hope the good moments continue to roll because football is such an important part of our social fabric. Long live our football!

Chapter 13
Rising stars affected by injuries and death

Obediah "Wasu" Sarupinda was a seasoned coach who had seen it all in the Rhodesia and later Zimbabwe Football fraternity. His football pedigree was also enhanced by the fact that he was a founder member of Dynamos Football club, one of the biggest football institutions in the country up to this day.

Wasu served Dynamos in various capacities as a coach and manager and transformed the club to the force that they are now. Together with Ashton "Papa" Nyazika and Lovemore "Mukadota" Nyabeza, he helped to build Dynamos fierce rivals Caps United and elevated them to the high table of football champions in 1979 when they clinched the league. A man of such football stature cannot be expected to be too excited when a new talent emerges.

Such wise old heads usually rely on the old age adage "Regai dzive shiri, mazai haana muto". Literally translated to "do not count your chickens before they hatch." But one Saturday morning in 1983, Wasu declared to the millions who read the back page of The Herald, "Come and see the next Archford Chimutanda!". He was referring to an emerging star, Edwin Farayi. Now, if a player was mentioned in the same breath as Archford Chimutanda in any capacity, then fans had every reason to pay attention. For indeed Archie was football royalty.

Fans were excited, but the excitement was shortlived because Farai soon suffered a career ending injury at the tender age of twenty-one. Cruel fate! Dear reader, there are many such young stars whose careers were disrupted by injuries, it is to them that I dedicate, with a heavy heart and a heavy pen this sad chapter.

Edwin Farai was good, very good and Wasu had every reason to be excited. Altough he was a defensive midfielder, one quality separated him from his peers, the eye for a pass. Edwin was a great passer of the ball and this is what drew comparison with Archford Chimutanda. When that clarion call was made by Wasu, fans flocked to Gwanzura Stadium. Caps United were playing Black Aces football club. Unfortunately, there was a downpour before the match and the poor drainage system meant that the match had to be abandoned. Was it a symbol? I am tempted to accept it as such because Edwin's dance with Zimbabwe football was shortlived.

A mere three years later, he suffered an ankle injury in a tackle by Clayton Munemo, a player whom you would not describe as a dirty player. It was an unfortunate tackle but, it marked the end of his career. But while he played he gave us some exciting moments. Was he as good Archie as suggested by the erstwhile coach? Well no one was as good as Archie, I think Wasu's hyperbole can be forgiven. Maybe with more time on the field of play, Edwin would have reached the apex of his career and come close to the master passer he was once compared to, we will never know.

"Who injured Samson Choruwa?" This is a never-ending debate, some even go further to ask, "Who bewitched Samson Choruwa?" The first question arises from the fact that many fans who claim to know the then twenty-year old attacking midfielder suggest that he was injured while playing "Money game".

"Money games" are informal games not sanctioned by the clubs, but which players engage in during the weekend or during the off-season. Injuries can occur, players often cover them up, come to the club, play a game while injured and then try to claim compensation. The second question is premised on the argument that no matter how he was injured, Samson's injury was not natural, fans claim that he was bewitched and the failure to recover explains the supernatural forces involved. Yes, we are Africans and such beliefs hold sway among us. However, let me not speculate. Let me go with the official record.

Samson "Sister" Choruwa announced himself in the year 2001 on the local football scene with some devastating displays for Dynamo Football Club. These were the days of the famed "Kidsnet Project" so named because the players were relatively young. Moses "Bambo" Chunga, the then Dynamos coach had the bravery to play the young boys at a club which has the most demanding supporters in the league. The supporters crave instant success and young players are bound to feel the pressure of playing for such a huge club. Chunga went against received wisdom and thrust these boys into action. What followed were some exciting displays and Samson became the fulcrum in this team of youngsters.

He played as an attacking midfielder and was well supported by the likes of Cephas Chimedza, Eddie Mashiri, Leo Kurauzvione and Norman Maroto among others. Samson was the star of the cast and I will always remember the goal he scored against Shabanie Mine in a league match at Rufaro Stadium. He exchanged passes with a colleague, dribbled past one defender, and feinted to shoot before curling the ball into the far corner of the goal.

I can still visualise it nearly twenty years later. I hope our National Broadcaster, the Zimbabwe Broadcasting Cooperation has a copy of this goal, it was of exceptional quality. I loved the goal because it was deliberately created, it was not an accident and it showed Samson as a thinking footballer. He deliberately initiated and crafted the move and the goal had his signature on it. What a way to announce yourself on the big stage. Cephas Chimedza his teammate at Dynamos told me that Choruwa had scored a similar goal against Amazulu in Bulawayo. I did not watch that one but after this goal, everyone knew about Samson Choruwa, a pattern of well crafted goals was developing. Then cruel fate intervened, injury struck!

In a match against Masvingo at Mucheke Stadium in 2002, Godfrey "Mai Mahofa" Dondo the Masvingo United captain lunged into a tackle which damaged Samason's knee. His career ended with that unfortunate tackle, Dynamos and Zimbabwe were deprived of a rising star. Though Godfrey Dondo later accepted that he had injured "Sister" as Choruwa was known by his peers, some fans claim that he simply exacerbated an injury which was already there. He was only 21 and despite numerous attempts to make a comeback, his efforts were in vain. His treatment regime might have been mismanaged with claims that Dynamos wanted to use a "Sangoma" to treat him rather take him to a knee specialist.

If that is the case, then it beggars' belief, the poor management of the injury gave rise to the supernatural and witchcraft theories which I hinted on above. What I know is that Dynamos' loss was the nation's loss. They should have managed this jewel better. Could he have been as good as his mentor Moses Chunga? We will never know but I am tempted to think that he could have come close. "Sister" was some talent!

At Caps United, I remember Basil Chisopo whose promising career was also cut short. Basil was a dribbling wizard and Charles Mabika, the ageless football commentator, gave him the moniker "Chisipo" for his slippery moves. He was a big loss for the club and the nation. His injury opened a can of worms as he took the club to court for compensation. It was a battle that he lost just like he lost the battle to come back to the game he loved.

Desmond "Gazza" Maringwa and Johannes "Signature" Ngodzo are among the greatest midfielders to emerge from our football fraternity. These two's great talents were never fully fulfilled because of the injuries that they suffered early in their careers. They were both injured while playing for the Zimbabwe national team. The injuries seemed innocuous at the time, but they proved to be stubborn.

Desmond Maringwa was injured in 2000 during a training session with the Zimbabwe National team on the eve of the Cosafa Cup Final. What made the injury even more difficult to stomach was the fact that he was about to move to Spain to join Celta Vigo in the La Liga. Speaking to The Herald, he said, "I had the opportunity to move to Cleta Vigo because they wanted a replacement for Claude Makelele who was leaving for Real Madrid and the coach had settled on me, everything was being sorted in the background." The injury changed everything and the dream of becoming the first Zimbabwe player to grace the Spanish league went up in smoke. Through sheer determination, Desmond was able to have a dogged career at Dynamos, but it is my firm belief that he deserved better. Without the injury, a career abroad was on the cards.

The same can be said about Johannes Ngodzo the man they called "Signature" for his silky ball skills. Ngodzo emerged with a bang at Higlanders Football club, he was a talent to behold and before long National team coach, Sunday Chidzambwa called him for national duty. In a match against Eriteria on 5 July 2003, Ngodzo went up for a high ball, controlled it but when he landed, he immediately collapsed to the floor. He tried to stand up but failed. After a long treatment on the pitch, he was whisked off but what had appeared to be an an innocuous attempt to control the ball marked the end of a great player. Ngodzo was an excellent player, Highlanders

Football Club lost a rising star, and Zimbabwe lost a potential legend. Ngodzo could have earned many caps in the green and gold of the Warriors. What a shame!

Another great player whose career was cut short was Richard "Dabuka" Choruma who played for Highlanders Football club as a midfielder. He was one of the most energetic midfielders to grace our league and the nickname Dabuka was the fans' tribute to this quality. "Dabuka" was synonymous with the electrification of the Dabuka to Harare Railway line, the new electric train was meant to be a game changer to the economy. In Richard, fans saw the ability to be a game changer hence the nickname. Then injury struck when he was reaching peak form at twenty-five and another great talent was lost.

Francis Madziwa was given the nickname "Mercedes Benz" by the Dynamos faithful. He had joined the team in 2002 from Sporting Lions and was known for his spell bounding performances from rightback. Then one day, while returning from an away match, there was an accident. Madziwa was sitting on the front seat and his legs were crushed.

He never recovered, and his budding career was cut short. It was a blow for Dynamos and the National Team, a huge loss! Dynamos Football Club did not exactly cover themselves in glory because they did little to help the player during his rehabilitation and maybe because there was not insured, he did not get compensated. What a shame. Musset Zengeni was also injured but his club refused to help him with his rehabilitation apparently because he incurred the injury while playing "a money game." The curse of the" money game" had struck again.

Others whose careers were cut short at a young age include Masimba Mambare, a very good attacking midfielder, Naison Machekela a midfielder, Heaven Chinyama a striker and Malvern Samaneka. All these players were below the age of thirty, some were just beginning others were reaching their peak. I have deliberately left out those who were over the age of thirty. I should not also forget Zhaimu Jambo who was reaching his peak at Kaiser Chiefs. Tragically the man who inflicted the injury on him was his best friend, Tinashe "Father" Nengomasha during a training session. It was an unfortunate injury although the two remain friends.

Death also cut the short the careers of several young risings stars. I know there is a chapter that I dedicated to departed legends and I mentioned the tragic deaths of Blessing Makunike, Gary Mashoko, Shngi Arlon and Watson Muhoni but let me add three more whose life was snuffed out just as their stars were beginning to shine. The circumstances of their death were tragic and will make even the heart of Pharoah melt.

Levy Mchulu was an upcoming goalkeeper for 1992 League Champions, Black Aces Football Club. Although he was largely regarded as the number two because of the form of first team goalkeeper Emmanuel "Shumba" ● Nyahuma, his talent was never in doubt and many tipped him to take over the number one shirt soon. Then one end of year Award giving celebration party changed everything. As is the norm at most clubs, the end of season award ceremony party is a highly anticipated event.

For the clubs, it is an opportunity to show appreciation to the players. Food and beverages will be in abundance and players can indulge themselves. Often because of the over indulgence, fatal decisions can be made. It happened with Levy who after the party decided to use public transport to go home in Tafara, a suburb near Mabvuku in Harare.

"His sister who was at the party noticed that Levy was drunk, she urged him to get a taxi home which would drop him right at his doorstep. She even gave him the taxi fare, but he had other ideas, he decided to use public transport, it proved fatal!" said Charles "Star Black" Kaseke his teammate at Black Aces in a recent discussion. As fate would have it, when he dropped off from the public transport, the one kilometre he had to walk to his parents' house proved to be his last. Robbers attacked him. They beat him up and left him for dead. When people eventually saw him in the morning, it was too late, the young goalkeeper was dead. How tragic!

Oscar Molife was regarded as one of the most talented schoolboy to emerge from the hotbed of talent, Churchill High school. Many premier league clubs were after his signature and before long he was on the books of CAPS United in 1994. He was tipped to be a star of the future and although he had to drop down a league with Zimbabwe Crackers, many felt that he would bounce back stronger and become a regular with Caps United. Then one day, on his way from a training session, he was attacked by robbers. They beat him up and left him to die. They murdered him in cold blood. I hate such people and in such cases I do not hesistate to support the death sentence for those who commit such violent crimes. Oscar, like Levy was a big loss, a flower just about to bloom but cruelly snatched from our midst.

Then there was Tutani "Toots" Moyo, one of the most talented players to emerge from the endless talent production factory headed by Ali Baba Dube at Highlanders. Indeed, Baba Dube is regarded as the doyen of junior football in Bulawayo and with Highlanders Football Club. He nurtured some unbelievable talent. Many great stars passed through his expert coaching and one of them was Tutani or "Toots" as he was known by his peers.

Technically, no-one in his age group matched him and he managed to play a few matches for a star-studded Highlanders. However, the competition for places in the midfield department was stiff and like other talented youngsters at this club, Toots had to move. He joined

Black Mambas a police club based in Harare in 1988. On the pitch, he was simply brilliant, off it he was bit reckless. A misunderstanding with a teammate over a woman proved to be his undoing. It was alleged that an axe was used to attack him, which left him paralysed. Wheelchair bound, his great talent was lost and eventually he succumbed to his injuries. Another big loss!

Indeed, injuries and death have ruined the careers of many up and coming stars and the football fraternity was robbed. Some injuries were poorly managed, the chances of recovery were lost. It is true that we need more trained personnel in the field of injury and recovery management and if this happens, when injuries strike our players, the opportunity of recovery will be enhanced. We need to up our game in this regard. Otherwise, we will continue to lose talented players like what we did with Samson Choruwa among others. We cannot allow this to continue!

Chapter 14
From "Kunyunya" to "Chibhubhubhu" ... Our own way of talking Football!

To say football is a universal language is an age-old cliché often repeated by every football fan, pundit and expert. However, no football story is the same. Each nation has its own unique way of experiencing football. With these unique experiences, a special language specific to a given nation, develops. I have talked about the unique skills that footballers in Zimbabwe have developed over the years, in the same breath let me also highlight the unique terms that we have often used to describe our football. I draw inspiration from Tom Williams masterpiece book, "Do you speak Football?" which covers eighty-nine countries and looks at seven hundred football terms. His list is expansive but not necessarily exhaustive, so let me contribute a few from Zimbabwe.

This will be interesting because all of us can relate to most of the terms. We came up with some of them as we played football in the streets and on the dusty pitches dotted around the country. Most of the terms that will make you smile, even laugh out loud at the sheer creativeness of it all.

This is a special chapter and a special chapter demands a different style. I will highlight a term and try to explain the meaning in English for the benefit of those who might not be familiar with the Shona or Ndebele version. Here we go!

1.   Kutumwa kumagirosa – this was a favourite of Mukoma Choga Tichatonga Gavhure one of

Zimbabwe 's best football commentators in the vernacular. He used it a lot to describe the body swerve or dummy which leaves an opponent going one way and the one with the ball another. It is a powerful image like sending someone to the shops without enough money, it is obvious the person will return with nothing because you cannot buy anything without enough cash. It is like being send on a fool's errand, a wild goose chase.

2. Sticken- Anyone who played football on the streets or the dusty pitches will be familiar with this one. Sticken was the mother of all disputed goals and many matches were abandoned over this. When we were growing up, we used improvised goal posts. These were made of two stones or bricks to represent the goalposts. If someone hit a shot and it went close the stone, the unanimous cry from the opposition team would be "sticken" meaning it has gone above the goal post. Arguments emanating from this scenario had the potential to end in fist fights and the abandoning of the match, for peace to prevail one team had to relent by either accepting that it was indeed "sticken". That was the only way out!

3. Kurohwa deya – many defenders fell victim to this humiliating dribbling skill by those blessed with audacious football skills. Boy Ndlovu the dribbling wizard who played for Eagles specialised in this. The world over it is known as the nutmeg.

4. Chibhubhu versus kuwaridza bhora - when people say "Paita chibhubhu" they simply mean that the team has resorted to kick and rush football, there is no formula, no attempt to construct any meaningful moves. The opposite of this is "Kuwaridza bhora or bhora pasi" which is to pass the ball on the grass, keeping it on the surface and

making an effort to put together a lot of passes. The more creative of football enthusiasts will shout "bhora pasi, ndenge mudenga" roughly translated to "keep the ball on the surface and let aeroplanes fly in the sky" This is the perfect way maybe of describing "carpet football" the Zimbabwean way!

5. Kunyunya, Kuwaura, Kutsvaira or in Ndebele reitsha – all these mean one thing, dribbling usually with devastating effect, leaving the defender for dead I have discussed the dribbling wizards who graced our local stadiums, with such words were they often associated.

6. Kupfekedzwa heti – in Brazil they call it the Chapeou and they often cite the skill displayed by the then seventeen-year old Pele at the 1958 world cup when he lifted the ball over the head of a defender before connecting with and hammering it home. That was an exquisite goal by an emerging talent of world football. In Zimbabwe any such move even if it does not result in a goal is referred to as "Kupfekwedzwa heti" making the victim wear a hat so to speak. This is humiliating or emasculating

7. 12 o'clock or hora – this one means the player has ballooned the ball over the bar, a hopeless attempt at goal. The ball disappears into the sky!

8. Mbama – it is one of the most devastating skills used by Zimbabwe players. It involves dragging the ball away from the defender in a half circle as the attacker evades the defender. Fans love this skill and the whole ground will respond.

9. Mhonya, Dandara, Mupinyi, Tsvimbo or Inkomo in Ndebele – these are abusive terms which are used to describe what are deemed to be hopeless players. Football fans can be cruel and such terms

reveal that mean streak which resides deep in the hearts of most fans.

10. Kutsika nyoka- I find this interesting because in Kenya they call it "kukanyanga nyoka" which is Swahili for "stepping on a snake ". In both instances it means a failed attempt to stop the ball by stepping on it. It is an interesting metaphor, it is as if the player will be afraid to step on the ball the same way one will be afraid to step on a snake.

11. Bhora Muhondo – when a coach suddenly decides to play this style, he will be looking for results by any means possible. In that case the elaborate passing and intricate moves will be suspended because at the earliest opportunity, the ball is launched upfront, into the danger zone, the eighteen-yard box. The idea will be to cause as much commotion as possible in the opposition box and hope for a goal to come by. It is a playing style which seeks results by constant bombardment of enemy territory. It is not the most beautiful style.

12. Mbashto, Juju, tsotso – the Zimbabwean football narrative cannot be complete without incidences of the supernatural to achieve results being mentioned. The extent to which individuals and teams go to achieve the desired results baffles me. Tendai Tanyanyiwa who used to play for Black Aces and Dynamos had this to say on his Face Book page "One day the Chairman of one club called me to this room. He showed his erect manhood and told me that I should come back in the morning to check. I went back in the morning and lo and behold the manhood was still erect! Whether it had been erect the whole night, I am not sure but he immediately told me that we were going to win one nil. Indeed, we won one nil beating out nearest rivals Highlanders. It was

unbelievable what we had to go through to win football matches, some of the rituals we had to endure, they make me sweat whenever I look back "This was not a one-off narration, he talked about many incidences. Indeed, there are many in the Zimbabwe football fraternity who still believe that a team cannot just win football matches. They believe that magic must be part of any match preparation, we call that juju, mbashto or tsotso!

13. Man On – in Argentina they call out "ladron" which can be translated to thief, a thief is trying to steal your ball. Well in the motherland we simply say "Man On to alert a teammate."

14. Chigunwe- an interesting description of the toe poke. In Zimbabwe it often meant literally poking the ball with one's toe because at some level players do not have football boots.

15. Chekuseri –this is a simple skill but very effective, pushing the ball past an opponent then meeting it on the other side leaving the defender stranded.

16. Kusiya Mari Mutsangadzi- a very elaborate way to explain a poor performance which results in defeat. In Zimbabwe, a defeat usually means that the players will not be paid, so "Kusiya mari mutsangadzi" means the bonuses have been left on the pitch.

17. Foreign based or Maprovovho - around 1991 these new words entered our football discourse. This was the time when players like Moses Chunga, Willard Khumalo and Henry Mackop were based abroad and when national duty called fans always asked, "Have the foreign based stars arrived?" Foreign based became a badge of honour and because they were full time professionals while some at home were still part time, we called them Maprovhovho a corruption of the term

professionals. Currently in the Zimbabwe football fraternity opinion is divided as to whether anyone at a foreign club especially in Europe should be called for National duty. During the Moses Chunga era we did not really care about the level of the league, we were just excited that players were coming from Europe. What level they were playing did not matter. The new generation of fans however have become more and more critical and analytic and want the players to be playing at a high level. Some prominent supporters like the late Freddy Pasuwa Mugadza and Dylan Choto are fierce critics of those who play in lower leagues in Europe which they derogatively refer to as "Church Leagues" or "cemetery leagues ". They feel that these should not get National Team call ups. Others however like Mystery Chipere who has gone to the extent of forming a group, Zimbabwe Foreign Legion is always fighting in the corner of these youngsters and wants them to be called for National duty. The two camps are worlds apart, but I hope Zimbabwe football will be the winner. We indeed need the "foreign based" but they must add value to our National team.

18. Chaunga – there was a time when stadiums used to be packed because of the quality of football at display. Nothing excites more that to see stadiums packed with the colours of the various teams, the blue and white of Dynamos, the black and white of Highlanders and even the green and white of Caps United. Nothing beats a packed stadium. We do not call this a crowd, in Zimbabwe we call it " chaunga." This word has a deep meaning, it denotes the contribution of the 12th man to any team. All players are inspired by a big crowd, some however get carried away and chose to play to the

185

gallery. Fans will say "Anotambira Chaunga ",
playing to the gallery!

19. Vietnam, Soweto – these terms are a reference to
the two stands which are synonymous with the
hardcore Dynamos and Highlander supporters at
Rufaro Stadium and Barbourfields respectively.
Dynamos supporters have long appropriated
Vietnam as their home base, they are vocal,
influential and can make or break a coach or a
player. If they do not like a certain player, they will
give him a torrid time and as a result many good
players have lost form. They are a force of good,
but they can also have a negative influence on the
team. The same can be said about the Soweto
Stand were mostly hardcore Highlanders
supporters congregate. Again, these supporters can
be a force for good because they deeply love the
team but when things go awry they can be violent
and tarnish the image of the club. Highlanders
Football Club and Dynamos Football Club have
often been slammed with heavy fines following the
violent behaviour of these sets of supporters. It is
true that there is a Vietnam mentality just as there
is a Soweto mentality, a mentality which can be
anti-football.

20. Pabonde, Kukwesha Bhenji – in Zimbabwe a
"Bonde "is a sleeping mat made of reeds, it can also
be a sitting mat. When a player is said to be sitting
"Pabonde" he will on the bench. A perennial bench
warmer is referred to as "vepabonde "or
"Anokwesha bhenji...." It is cruel!

21. Shinda, Mbarure, Mupfondo, Mbambande, Museve –
all terms denote a powerful shot. Many players
were renowned for this, players such as Shaw
Handriade, Shepherd Muradzikwa, David Zulu,
David Mwanza, Misheck Makota and Elvis Chiweshe

to mention a few who were renowned for their powerful shots!

22. Kuhwishura- is simply to miss the ball completely, an air-short.

23. Chidobi – is an exquisite skill.

24. Kufemera mugotsi- many defenders were renowned for tight marking. One such defender was Dumisani "Commando" Mpofu who played for Blackpool, Caps United and the Zimbabwe National team. He never gave a striker any breathing space and he was the personification of "Kufemera mugotsi", tight marking. It is an interesting description.

25. Cheko – is a reference to that technique of bending the ball around the keeper, hitting a curling shot.

26. Pamutomato, Mugadzikwa – this is an interesting description of the penalty spot, only the person who came up with this one can explain it. Mugadzikwa however is easy to explain, it captures the process of putting the ball on the penalty spot. It however suggests that taking a penalty is easy, that scoring from the spot is given but nothing can be further from the truth!

27. Ku Stitcher- this denotes very skilful players who can knit together passes. If a team can play a passing style, putting together a number of passes we also use this term to describe it. Alternatively, "mushina wemajuzi," knitting a jersey is used as well to capture this style.

28. Gemazo, Zhale – is slang for a football match. We are going "KuGemazo" simply means we are going to watch football. "Zhale" is also a popular term for a football match.

29. Kumisa Zvidhori – this is an interesting one which describes a coach's ability to put the right players in

the best position and to come up with a winning formula. If a coach fails to do that people will say "akadhakwa" roughly translated to "He is drunk", he does not know what he is doing. A good coach should be able to make use of the playing resources at his disposal.

30. Kuchunira, Kubheura- this is a badge of shame! Many defenders are renowned for scoring own goals. Very good defenders have suffered this humiliation of picking the ball from their own net and wishing that that pitch would swallow them. Fans call this kuchunira or kubheura, scoring an own goal.

31. Upfu Musauti – this was introduced into our football discourse by none other than legendary commentator Mukoma Choga Gavhure. It was his own special way of describing a player caught offside. It is both funny and creative, putting salt into mealie meal, funny!

32. Kugeza nebhora, Kuwacha, kubvinza maoko – the scrutiny is often on goalkeepers and any blunder can be costly. These terms refer to that moment when goalkeepers develop butter fingers and make howlers which result in a goal. Two goalkeepers in our football history will forever be associated with this, John Sibanda against Congo Brazzaville in 1991. A harmless looking cross, and poor old John dropped it into his own net. It was the mother of all howlers and the whole Nation cried. Then came Elvis Chipezeze at Afcon 2019, I bet he still has nightmares about that match against DR Congo. Some of the mistakes that Elvis made in one match are literally impossible to believe!

33. Kutengesa Mutambo, Kusechesa – this is often about suspected match fixing. When a goal is conceded in dubious circumstances, a player can be

accused of selling the match. There were such accusations especially of goalkeepers like Bruce Grobelaaar, George Chigova and even Elvis Chipezeze. Often these players are often accused of being bought or being involved in some betting syndicates. They were called "Dyise" literally translated to sellouts.

34. Nyanga – to rise majestically and head the ball home. Makwinji Soma Phiri who played for Highlanders and Dynamos was known for his heading ability, "Ndeve nyanga" fans used to say, meaning he is very good with his head.

35. Kudhiza – like in all spheres of life, football is also susceptible to corruption. It has been alleged and many players have confessed to this, that some coaches demand payments in the form of cash or gifts from players. It is palm greasing of the coach and I am sorry to say that many veteran coaches have been accused of engaging in this obnoxious behaviour. Makes me wonder about a coach who was nicknamed "Dhiza", was the nickname a product of this ill behaviour. That might be well worth investigating. Payments can also be made to referees and it is easy to tell when "Muzvinapembe", the referee has been bought. When money has changed hands, many dubious decisions are made. This kills football and must be fought with all the weapons at our disposal.

36. Zviponda meso – this is anti football, boring, boring football, nothing to write home about.

37. Kunyima, anonyima – this is used to describe selfish players, they will never pass the ball to a better positioned player.

38. Tsono- defence splitting pass, many players were renowned for these, midfielders like Moses

Chunga, Stix Mtizwa, Isaac Riyano and Archford Chimutanda to mention a few.

39. Keke – this is the perfect pass, the perfect ball played to a striker and literally begging to be converted into a goal. Archford Chimutanda used to be a master of these and he always boasted, "Tinokupai makeke. We give you cakes." Another player who had that panache of giving "Keke" was Nkulumo Donga, he always gave the ball on a silver platter! "Keke" Is the Shona version of the of the word cake.

40. Kudzinga Mhashu – a powerful metaphor meaning chasing away the locusts. This is often used for the reserve sides or curtain raisers and the idea is that as they play before the main match they drive off the "grasshoppers "in readiness for the main match.

41. Nguva yemaranjisi – the assumption was that at halftime, players were given loads of oranges to replenish their bodies. Indeed, the teams often carried sacks of oranges as they entered the stadiums. Even at schools and grassroots level, oranges were the staple diet at halftime, so it became the norm to call halftime "time yemaranjisi oranges time"

42. Kukwata Gemu – bhora - another interesting metaphor, anyone who has ever cooked sadza a staple diet in Zimbabwe knows what "Kukwata" is. Now if a player is accused of "Kukwata bhora, it is to be accused of cowardice, it is cardinal sin, hiding on the pitch. Fans are not amused by such players.

43. Kuma Zigo – this is a Highfield special, a special dedication from the old suburb also known as Fio in street language. KumaZigo is a tribute to the iconic Zimbabwe Grounds which are situated right in the heart of the suburb. These grounds groomed

190

many players, they were the epicentre of grassroots football. The grounds are a rite of passage, anyone who grew up in Highfield spent time on these four pitches. Sadly, they are now dilapidated and have been neglected but they remain a place of hope for many Highfield residents. Hopefully the next big star will emerge from these dusty pitches, kuma Zigo!

44. iBosso ngenkani – no football declaration in Zimbabwe is made with so much conviction, it simply means " Bosso, Highlanders Football Club till I die.!" The declaration captures the meaning of this iconic institution to the fans.

45. Seven Million - this is the purpoted number of fans who follow Dynamos Football club. Interestingly this figure was arrived at when the Zimbabwe National population was seven million in 1980. It was cheeky therefore for the Dynamos fans to claim that the whole population belonged to them. Fortunately, their claimed figure has not changed, they still call themselves Seven million despite the current population now standing at 14 million!

46. Bhora harinyebe – this is a former Caps United and Harare City coach Lloyd Chitembwe special. This statement is loaded with meaning, it means that if you do not do the right thing when training and preparing for a match, the players and the team will be exposed on match day. If a player has been cutting corners at training his limitations will come out on match day. A coach who fails to prepare the team adequately will not be able to hide the weaknesses of his team on the pitch.

"Bhora Harinyebe!" Dear reader, do you want a literal translation? I guess you do, it means "Football does not lie." In football, you reap what you sow! This was a powerful message. Our football leaders should also accept this free wisdom. To be a football Nation of note, proper structures, support and planning should be in place. You cannot just wake up one day and become a powerhouse, planning and preparation is key!

As posited in the introduction, no football experience is the same and indeed every football experience gives rise to unique words and statements in the football discourse. In Argentina they added "Mano De Dios", referring to the Diego Maradona 'Hand of God' of 1986. The Germans still talk about the "Wembley Tor" referring to the dubious England goal in the 1966 World Cup. These are among the special terms that are highlighted in Williams' book. In the same breath, I hope I have done justice to our own special football language in this discussion. I think all of us can relate and although the list is not exhaustive, it is gives us a starting point!

Chapter 15
Local is lekker, let us bring back the Glory!

When I started on this football journey, "Local was truly lekker" to borrow an adage
from our neighbours South Africa. The excitement generated by the local league had no rival, the fans' total commitment was to the local teams and the local heroes. While I accept that fans knew about such great global powerhouses like Liverpool, Manchester United, Tottenham, Arsenal, Nottingham Forest, these teams did not generate as much interest as teams such as Dynamos, Caps United, Highlanders, Gweru United, Black Rhinos, and Black Aces, among others.

Yes, we knew about John Barnes, Ian Rush, Kenny Dalgish and other world stars but for a true relationship with football heroes it was to the likes of Shambo, Tauro, Madinda, Maronga, Kateya, Chimutanda among others that fans turned their attention. With these players, we had a very special relationship. They were our stars, our heroes! However, the momentum has shifted, the interest in the local game has dissipated, most of us now lack conviction in our league, our heroes have become the likes of Messi and Ronaldo.

The teams that have captured our hearts are those from faraway leagues. The local league has become a footnote in our football discussions with the English Premier League, La Liga, Bundesliga and the Italian League taking centre stage in most discussions. Those of a certain age like myself are filled with nostalgia of the past and see nothing good in the current generation while the fans of a younger generation see nothing good in the current crop of players and escape to European leagues to satiate their football hunger.

As a result, stadiums are almost empty except for very special matches and internationals. I worry for the future of our local league and I keep asking myself, when did this rain begin to beat us? How can we recapture the lost glory, how can we regenerate that lost interest? How can we declare again that Local is lekker? These are real existential questions and they need to be answered.

We used to fill stadiums by mid-day for the traditional 3pm kick off on Saturday or Sunday. I remember one Chibuku Trophy final in 1982 between Dynamos and Caps United. Imagine a Dynamos line up with Japhet Mparutsa, Oliver Kateya, Misheck Marimo, Sunday Marimo, David Mandigora, Hamid Dhana, July Sharara, Kembo Chunga, Edward Katsvere and yes, the man himself the evergreen Archford "Chehuchi" Chimutanda, this was the crème-de-la crème of Zimbabwe football.

On this derby day they had to face Duncan Ellison, David Gwanzura, Size Torindo, Charles Sibanda, William Chikauro, Joel Shambo, the evergreen Stix Mtizwa, Stanley Ndunduma, goal machine Shacky Tauro and the powerful Friday Phiri, this was a battle to savour. The excitement generated by this encounter shot through the roof. It meant one had to be in the stadium by 12 pm or risk missing the match. Rufaro Stadium has a capacity of thirty-five thousand people, but on this sundrenched Sunday afternoon, I dare say forty thousand squeezed themselves in like sardines into this spiritual home of Zimbabwe football.

What followed was a football match made in heaven, drama, twists and turns, skills galore and a midfield performance by the midfield maestro Chimutanda which left his fellow artists in the department, Shambo and Mtizwa, outran and outmanoeuvred.

Ten thousand miles away in England, Liverpool were being crowned champions of the English first Division and Aston Villa were beating Bayern Munich to win the European Cup. Did this really matter to us? Did this grab the headlines in our local newspapers? The answer dear reader is no. Why? Our football was good enough to absorb all our attention. Football "gods" so to speak used to inhabit our football arenas. Our hearts were fully persuaded, our loyalty undivided, and our emotional attachment was with the local heroes.

There were many such matches which attracted capacity crowds in our football terrain. Rufaro, Gwanzura, Barbourfiled, Ascot, Cam and Motor, Luveve, Torwood, Sakubva stadiums, they used to be packed to the brim as fans thronged to watch their local heroes. The giant National Sports Stadium often hosted the Cup finals, the champions league and the National team matches which would often be filled to near capacity.

During the magical Dream Team days, it was the norm to have capacity crowds of sixty thousand fans. At one stage Dynamos hosted Asec Mimmosa of Ivory Coast, the stadium was packed to the brim. Fans looked forward to the weekend, in every major town, the routine was the same. The football culture was really embedded in the fans, many lived for the weekend and the weekend was all about football. It comes as a shock for me therefore when at this juncture we have Dynamos playing a match in a half empty stadium. Some games now attract a crowd of less than one hundred people. I consider this to be an abomination. It is heartbreaking to see players giving their all-in a near-empty stadium with the sound of their own voices and the referee's whistle.

Players need fans and we should work hard to bring the fans back. But we need to know how the problem came upon us and try to cure this disease. It will not be an easy cure for indeed a disease which has never been seen before cannot be treated with every day herbs. The disease has been festering and we have watched it fester, now we need very strong medicine to cure it.

The biggest challenge that we are facing as a football nation is the economy which has affected the operations of many clubs. As earlier pointed out, many teams have folded especially those which were sponsored by individuals and companies. Indeed, the Zimbabwe football terrain is signposted with many who travelled the road but fell by the wayside. The mine teams like Mhangura, Shabanie, Ziscosteel, Rio Tinto have all disappeared because the operation at most mines, their chief sponsors became unsustainable. This led not only to the demise of sporting facilities, but also the talent which used to emerge from these mining communities. Many great players were produced from these communities and the demise of the mines impacted the production chain of players in a massive way. Where will the next Joseph Zulu, Charles Chirwa, Ephert Lungu, James Takawada, Thomas Makwasha among others come from? The sporting facilities in these communities were top notch and often motivated many young men to play football.

Many players were offered apprenticeships to train as fitter and turners, boiler makers and mechanics. This ensured that many of them decided to stay with these mining teams thereby making them very competitive. The harsh economic environment put paid to all this and many of the facilities are now in a sorry state.

An environment motivates the young when sporting facilities are in place. Many young people will stay off the streets, off drugs and more talent emerges. This is no longer the case, many young people have resorted to substance abuse while others have joined the gold panning craze which has gripped the country. The motivation to play football is no longer there and this is compounded by the fact that football does not pay anymore. Potentially massively talented players have been lost to other activities. When the young people stop dreaming, the Nation perishes. Football has not been spared this death of dreams!

It is sad to read about players spending months and months without being paid and when they boycott matches, they are portrayed as mercenaries. In the past, players were not paid a lot but most of them were able to supplement their football incomes by going to work. Currently, players are considered professionals. They depend on football for an income, but what do they get? They get peanuts at best, and at worst months without pay. It is a shame.

The problem is widespread among some of the smaller clubs in our league with only a few managing to keep their players happy by paying them on time. The problem points to the economy and it is important to restore our country to functionality. Without this it will be difficult for clubs to operate well. Of course, clubs should also think outside the box and find ways to generate extra income.

They should market their brands better by selling regalia to supporters. One of Dynamos' top supporters, the now late Freddy Pasuwa Mugadza, believed that clubs can generate thousands of dollars through innovative thinking like opening food courts, hotels, opening sports shops and making sure that the selling of club regalia is done through the right channels. I believe that this is possible but that needs a leadership that is committed to professionalism.Overall, I think if we fix the economy, a conducive atmosphere will exist for football to thrive. The game of football should be professional in the true sense of the word so that players can make a career out of it. It is important to retain players if our league is to continue being respectable. When I started on this journey in the 1980s very few players went outside the country to play.

Yes, I have also argued that there are many who deserved to play abroad if the chance had come, but I think the quality would not have been affected because there were so many good players. These days however, player retention is difficult. The South African league quickly snatches any player who shows signs of talent. The star players are quickly lost and not replaced so the quality of play continues to go down. This is the challenge which we are facing, how to improve the quality without necessarily blocking those who want to move from moving. Maybe we would not have to worry about the quality going down because the departed stars would easily be replaced if we had junior structures.

Most of our teams have abandoned the junior structures citing the harsh economic environment. Teams such as Highlanders, Dynamos and Platinum still have some reserve sides, but most teams simply cannot be bothered. In the past, clubs produced stars who were quickly promoted to senior teams. I remember at one point, Caps United promoting the likes of Gift Mudangwe, Tobias Sibanda, Silver Chigwenje, Joe Mugabe, and Oscar Motsi into the first team. This was an exciting time for the club and the departure of veterans was not fatal.

Supporters continued to sing songs of joy because the new kids on the block delivered some scintillating displays. It is always nice when young players come on board. Teams should therefore revert to this policy of producing young stars and unleashing them in the league. This keeps the excitement levels at an optimum and keeps the league strong. When a league is strong, when good players keep emerging, fans come to the stadiums. If a culture of good football is developed, soon the fans will believe again in the league and come back home.

Indeed, the fans need to come back because now most of them are disillusioned and some are literally captured by leagues afar. They are disillusioned because the general perception is that the local quality has gone down, that the league has been reduced to an eyesore due to the mediocre talent and poor management. Many fans who grew up in an era of big stars compare the current players and find nothing to admire.

They dismiss the current crop as not fit enough to tie the laces of those former greats. I admit that there was a time when we were spoilt for choice in terms of quality, but I do not believe that the current crop is beyond redemption. I believe that we need to give them a chance to prove their worth and the only way to do that is to give them the moral support. Attending football matches is the small contribution that fans can make.

As fans, we should also avoid creating a vicious cycle of negativity because of our endless negative perceptions. While accepting that the situation is not right, we cannot declare that football is dead. It is our duty to keep it alive or if we think it is dead, then we should try and resurrect it. The fans must come back, it is a fact that many are now captured by the growth of the English Premier league, the La Liga and the Bundesliga which have captured their hearts. Exposure to televised games has opened the eyes of fans to the highest levels of competitive football.

When they come back from these televised games, they see nothing good in their local players. This is a big challenge in most African leagues, the fans no longer believe, faith has been lost. Zimbabwe football's saving grace is that we still have the traditional giants in existence. Dynamos and Highlanders are more than football clubs, they remain a way of life for many loyal fans. As long as these teams are alive, the league will not be starved of its oxygen. Caps United also retain a strong loyal fan base and therefore all hope is not lost. What these clubs must do is to put their houses in order, develop good players and play good football and the fans will come for games. When Dynamos play well, the fans come to watch good game, the same applies to Highlanders. Bulawayo comes to life whenever Bosso is playing. If companies sponsored teams like Platinum, Ngezi Platinum and ZPC Kariba so they can continue to exist and play good football, then the fans will come back.

It is also important to improve the sponsorship in the league. While I appreciate that companies like National Breweries have been faithful football partners, it is important to have more similar partners inorder to increase the value. There would be no problem in inviting other players to help in sponsoring the league. Currently, most teams struggle because the money that they spend while travelling to and from matches is more than the money available in the league. The accommodation expenses and the winning bonuses can be overwhelming. As result, many struggled to finish the season and it is these viability challenges that must be addressed by engaging multiple sponsors. Natbrew therefore, should allow others to participate because a rich league will mean more sponsorship and less financial struggles for clubs, these make players stay and teams becomes stronger. With that, fans will come back, and the glory years can be rediscovered.

The Zimbabwe Football Association should also show good leadership in guiding the football ship. It is my hope that one day we will have more former footballers like Lichon Mutasa leading the game. I cite Linchon Mutasa because he showed great vision when he led Dynamos. He was able to invest in a Sports shop and to buy a piece of land for the club. If he had been allowed to continue, I think Dynamos could have been transformed from a sleeping giant into a proper giant. Football has become big business. It is possible to grow this business if we have the right leadership and who better to lead the industry if not former players (legends). These former legends have a passion for football, there are many who have exposure in business who should be allowed the opportunity to lead.

While I call for sponsorship to increase, I am also aware that the fans must reciprocate. They need to come to the stadiums to support their teams and not cause problems. Indeed, Zimbabwe football often suffers from the curse of hooliganism. Fans from the big clubs, Highlanders, Dynamos and Caps United often find it difficult to accept defeat. They often resort to missile throwing and worse still, uncouth behaviour when their teams lose. Often enough, matches have been abandoned due to the mayhem caused by these fans. On many occasions, the beautiful Barbourfields Stadium has been turned into a war zone by Highlanders diehards. Rufaro Stadium, and even the National Sports Stadium, have all been turned into arenas of shame in the past, by supporters who just could not accept defeat. Often enough, they blame refereeing decisions.

While I accept that decisions can be dubious, this should never be used as an excuse for mayhem. We need to stamp out this scourge even if it means making teams play their matches in empty stadiums. This will hurt the club, but I think this will make the hooligans sit down and reflect before embarking on their destructive path. Deducting points, banning well-known hooligans and closing pubs in the vicinity of stadiums on match days to reduce the pre-match ritual of drinking excessively will go a long way in reducing this football cancer. Education, it is key, clubs should educate their fans, they must make them aware of damage they do to the brand they support by engaging in violent acts.

As I write, there is a lot of excitement about the restoration of our football stadiums. The level of dilapidation has been shocking in stadiums like Chibuku, Gwanzura, Amaveni, Cam and Motor, Rufaro, Dzivarasekwa stadium and Glen Norah. The powers that be watched as stadiums became ghost facilities. I think the councils which are responsible for these facilities should do more to restore them to their glory. It is important to modernise these stadiums so that fans can feel safe to attend as families. The safety of fans and players should be paramount, and it is therefore important to drag our stadiums from the Stone Age era in which they are currently situated.

When we have good stadiums, we will increase our chances of hosting tournaments such as the Confederation of Southern Africa Football Associations (Cosafa) and the African Cup of Nations (Afcon), thereby helping to grow the game in the country. It is sad that the last time we tried to host the prestigious Afcon tournament was in the year 2000 and we lost because the quality of our stadiums was deemed substandard.

The stadiums that had been earmarked to host some of the matches were lagging in developments. We cried foul as a Nation pointing a finger at the then Confederation of African Football leader Issa Hayatou whom we believed had an axe to grind with us. Having lost the hosting rights, we took our eyes off the ball and allowed most of our stadiums to dilapidate. We made no effort to modernise and when so-called renovations were made on some of them, there was no noticeable difference. Money was spent but nothing changed with the stadiums. This clearly showed a lack of leadership from those who lead our football institutions and City Councils. Ironically, the renovations at Sakubva Stadium which started sometime in the year 2000 are only being completed in 2020. How is that for a serious football nation? I hope the momentum that we are currently seeing in fixing the stadiums will not run out of steam because most things in our country have had this history.

As I end this football narrative, it will be amiss not to give advice to the young players who have the future of

Zimbabwe football in their hands and feet. My grandmother Mbuya Mutsvuku repeated the same advice to anyone who cared to listen. "Usagarire maoko!, Do not sit on your hands !" She knew what she was taking about. Allow me to give the same advice to the up and coming stars. Nothing good will come from just sitting and waiting for a miracle. Hardwork is key! It is important to focus on both education and football. Football is a short career and a fallback plan is a good. Football players do not live in a vacuum, the same challenges that other young people face also affects them. Challenges such as substance abuse which is now very prominent among young people in our country.Like all young people it is important to avoid these. They should instead spend more time in the gyms which are now easily accessible to improve their stamina and physique.

They should also spend more time honing their skills, self motivation is key and is often the difference between a half decent player and a great one. It is dedication, focus and a desire to be the best which made great players great, if our players remember this then they will look after their bodies and make the most of their talents. My wish is to see great players emerge from our league who can make the league as exciting as when I started this journey.

I want to see great players who can conquer the world emerging from the Zimbabwe league. This is very possible although I accept that there are many rivers to cross before we get there. We have had great players who managed to leave their mark on the international scene, the likes of Peter Ndlovu, Benjani Mwaruwaru and now Marvellous Nakamba and Tino Kadewere. We need to revive that production line, so we can also raise our flag in the world. The more quality we produce, the better our league will be and the more we grow as a football nation.

The First Cut! Caps United will always be my team and I remain committed to the Zimbabwe league, I hope to see it grow in my lifetime. I cast envious glances at our neighbours Zambia and South Africa who are running rewarding league and keep improving their stadiums. Football in our country is not dead but is like a child fed grudgingly by cruel step parent. It is malnourished, and we need to act now to restore it to good health.

I envy the organisation of the Soweto derby in South Africa, which still commands record crowds of eighty thousand fans and is sold out two weeks before kickoff. My heart is filled with joy when I see great African players, over the years, leaving their mark on great clubs like Liverpool, Barcelona and Chelsea. Yes, there is no way that I can ignore the global nature of football, so Arsenal and Barcelona have often set my heart racing. However, after everything has been said and done, I still return to the first love. Zimbabwe football must grow, Zimbabwe clubs must be known throughout the world, we have to fight hard to make this happen. It will be a great day if I see a die hjard scouser wearing a Dynamos replica shirt or a Brazilian proud of his Highlanders shirt. Only then will I know that we have made strides. We need to take Zimbabwe Football to the world. I have a Dream, Yes we can!

Lest I forget, I still call myself a 'Shamboist'. It is a self coined term which is a tribute to the man who made me love football, Joel "Jubilee, The Headmaster" Shambo. Many heroes have come, many heroes have left, but Shambo will always have a special place in my heart. He made me believe.

I say, "Long live Zimbabwe football!"

References

1. William, T. (2018) *Do You Speak Football? A glossary of football words and phrases from around the world*, London: Bloomsbury Sport

2. Mucherahowa, M. (2017) *Soul of Seven Million Dreams, The Memory Mucherahowa Story*, Harare: Create Space independent publishing Platform

3. Paton, A. (2003) *Cry, The Beloved Country*. London: Jonathan Cape

Printed in Poland
by Amazon Fulfillment
Poland Sp. z o.o., Wrocław

61228598R00127